Purchase Knob

Purchase Knob

Essays from a Mountain Notebook

Kathryn K. McNeil
illustrated by Susan Renfrew

FITHIAN PRESS • SANTA BARBARA, 1999

Fithian Press
A division of Daniel and Daniel, Publishers, Inc.
Post Office Box 1525
Santa Barbara, CA 93102

Book design: Eric Larson

LIBRARY OF CONGRESS CATALOGING-IN-PUBLICATION DATA
McNeil, Kathryn K., (date)
    Purchase Knob : essays from a mountain notebook / Kathryn K. McNeil ;
illustrated by Susan Renfrew
        p.   cm.
    ISBN 1-56474-279-2 (alk. paper)
    1. Appalachian Region, Southern—Social life and customs. 2. Appalachian
Region, Southern—Biography. 3. Country life—Appalachian Region, Southern.
4. McNeil, Kathryn K., (date). 5. Natural history—Appalachian Region, Southern.
I. Title.
F217.A65M4   1999
974—dc21   98-33508
                                                              CIP

To Ernest, Bonnie and George
mountain friends forever

Contents

At last, out of the still blazing monotony of the piedmont pine woods in the heavy southern June rose the first trembling mirage of the mountains, the Blue Ridge, uplifting a 1,000-mile wall of granite, and beyond it, written in a gray, dream scrawl upon the sky, the Great Smokies.

—*Andre Michaux, 1787*

The House

THERE'S a summer place, a farm, forever imprinted on my memory, spacious in its views, lovely in its close-ups, on the gentle slopes of Purchase Mountain in the southern Appalachians. I built a house there at 5,000 feet. That's high for these parts. Mt. Mitchell, not far from me, is 1,600 feet higher. It's the highest point on the eastern seaboard between Mississippi and the Atlantic Ocean. These Appalachians are ancient mountains, some of the oldest on earth. Worn down by the ages from water, frost and the work of the wind, they are gentle, livable mountains. Having a home on top of one is as close to heaven as you can get.

Almost 600 acres, the farm is divided between meadows and forest. Two miles of unpaved road picks up where the county road stops, and leads you up another 1,000 feet through woods, across streams, until you suddenly drive from deep shade into sunlight and a mountain of grass flowing up in front of you, all the way to the very top. The house sits there, and it looks out over the whole world. It's hard to keep your eyes on the road this last stretch, there are so many mountains poking up on both sides of it, and more behind them. On a good clear day in October, there are 100 miles of mountains to see. Guests coming for their first-time visits virtually leap out of their cars when they reach the top. Could be their radiators are boiling over from the steady climb. Most times, though, I think they feel exuberant over where they are.

"You didn't tell us you lived on top of the world," they say, staring north, south, east. The forest behind me keeps them from looking west.

I smile and greet them, and deep down inside I get that same old thrill all over again I had when I saw their view for the first time myself.

It was one of those love-at-first-sight purchases. We rounded that same bend on the old wagon road, my husband and I, coming out of the woods to see the meadows before us with a warm June wind bending the grasses and the mountains all around. The road ran out, and I remember we got out and walked. We walked for hours just looking. We found an old cabin and broken-down barn and a year-round spring we could use for our water supply. We walked through forests of sweet gum and buckeyes and maples and found trillium blooming in the damp spots, and chestnut stumps four feet across. What a place for children. We had five of them. Here they could wander to their hearts' content. An occasional brown bear might cross their paths, or a rattler, but that was part of the wildness we loved about it all.

"I don't really want to sell the Purchase," Med Leatherwood told us, looking us over. This had been the name of the property for a hundred years. I don't know what he expected to see. Maybe our youth and enthusiasm helped, or maybe he was impressed that we had taken time to walk over it so fast. I had left a two-week-old baby at home in our eagerness to see it. I can still see Med in his bib overalls, his old brown felt hat pulled down over his eyebrows, speculating as he studied us about what kind of neighbors we'd make. He made us feel as if he were giving us a gift, despite the sizable check he was about to pocket. But he became our best friend, and we continued to let him pasture his cattle on the land. He'd remind us, though, once in a while when he came up to salt the cows, how lucky we were. He'd sit on our porch, studying the view, and shake his head.

"Shouldn't have sold it; it's too pretty," he'd say. Then he'd watch Suzy galloping over the grass on her horse, or eat one of the cookies Katy had just made, and he'd smile and say, "It was time."

We wanted a mountain architect to design the house, and we picked Charlie Sappenfield of Asheville. In 1964 he was young, like us. Unlike us, he smoked and was out of breath as we led him all over the property to possible house sites, each a nice heart-pounding climb from the one before. He trailed behind us, his raincoat flapping around his tall, lean frame.

"You couldn't do better than this one," he gasped from the spot we finally picked on the slopes of Limby Birch Mountain.

He was right. The site was naturally level, treeless, and covered in acres of wild mountain grass that spilled downhill on three sides until it met the forest. Purchase Knob, our own little mountain 5,400 feet

high, sat right out in front. It had a certain dignity of its own, having its name on all the topo maps of the area. Charles would frame it for us in the big window of the living room.

In seven months we had a house that was worthy of the land. It looked like a modified A-frame with a high, peaked roof sheltering the twenty-foot picture window. Stained gray, the house had a nice contrast of light and shade from the board-and-batten design of its wooden walls. Outrigger rafters protruded beyond the roof line and increased the play of light and shadow.

A wide porch cantilevered out over the grass and wrapped around the house on two sides. A chimney of field stones, salvaged from the barn below, rose into the sky. We entered under an extended roof line, a "breezeway," that connected the house with the garage and led into a sunny patio. The mountain men building the house through the cold winter months chuckled over that title on the house plans. "No breezes around here in December, January or February," they laughed. "More like tornadoes." They were sturdy, dependable builders who hurried to get the roof on and the fireplace built so they could be warm and dry all winter while they finished the insides. I got to know them on my weekly trips through that winter from our home in the Sandhills, 200 miles away.

I think they liked the place. I'd see them eating their lunches, sitting on the roughed-in window seat, looking at the Knob in October with its covering of golden hickory trees, or in January when ice fogs held the house with wet tentacles, they sat by the fire. In March, they worked in shirtsleeves while the sun poured through the high window, though the temperature hovered around freezing outside.

Sometimes I spent the night in the valley below at a motel so I could have a full day at the house with the workmen. One of these times I particularly remember. It was a morning that was bitterly cold. A winter fog lay heavy on the land and reached up into all the nooks and coves of the mountains. When I reached 4,000 feet, I began to drive out of it. Around a few more curves of the road and I was in bright sunlight, the house too. One of the carpenters stood on the porch looking out at the sea of fog below him, as far as the eye could see, with only the tops of the mountains floating like islands above it. His name was Andy. He was a coon hunter and he was building my kitchen cabinets this week. I liked him. Andy was an expert with his ruler and his saw, and he wanted to please me. I walked out on the porch to say good morning to him.

"Pretty sight, isn't it?" I said, wrapping my woolen scarf more tightly around my neck. It was 9:00 A.M. and about thirty degrees in the sun.

"Reminds me of the Indian Ocean," he said, giving me a nod and returning to the view.

What could a mountain man know of such a faraway place, I wondered. "What makes you say that?" I asked.

"I was stationed out there during the war, with the Seabees," he said. "Haven't seen anything since like it, till today." He turned to me and knocked the ashes out of his pipe. "Want to see those cabinets?"

Right after the roof went on, I made my weekly visit and walked inside. I was dismayed at what I saw. We were building a church, not a home! The roof was too high, and with its four rows of scissor beams the long fifty-foot room only lacked an altar in front of the high window.

Al, the head carpenter, reassured me.

"Wait. When we cut out the floor around the fireplace, you'll see a complete change."

He was talking about the "conversation pit," an idea of Sapenfield's that would break up the long, lean look of the room. A week later, when I returned, the church had become a home. Around the hearth now was a sunken twelve-foot square with two steps down to it from either side. Soft, lazy, built-in couches would one day soon fill in the three sides facing the fireplace, with a wall-to-wall carpet underneath them.

In time this room became a place for all ages and activities. Soup might be simmering away on the stove in the kitchen corner and the long harvest table set for lunch. Children could work on a jigsaw puzzle on the round table in the window, and others stretch out reading on the window seat. Cooking, visiting, cloud-watching, all became part of daily life in this high-ceiling room. Outdoors, beyond the porch, the mountains and sky filled up the glass doors and picture windows. Whatever was happening weather-wise outside was never missed by those inside.

The house can sleep fifteen and has many times. I've even taken in lost hikers and their guide late at night and put them to sleep on the couches. There's a loft with two rooms over the living room, with a balcony, that sleeps ten. My bedroom is off the big room, with a fireplace that backs up against the one in the living room. Old chestnut rafters from the barn cross my ceiling, the old adze marks still on them. My windows, too, are full of mountains and starlight. It's too pretty to pull the drapes, so I never do, and wake up at dawn most days with the red glow of sunrise filling the room and promising me another day of just being there.

A lot happens in thirty years. People change, interests change. My husband and I parted, each of us going our separate ways. I know he loved the Purchase, but he was restless there, and the place too quiet, and a lot of other things, bigger things, came between us. So I sleep alone there now. Our children are grown, and their children are walking the trails and climbing the Knob and watching the weather change and the great thunderheads sweep in from the west, bringing rain. The house welcomes all of us and endures. There isn't a time that I don't thrill to return to it. Even after the most tedious of errands to the town below or after months of absence, "I'm back again," I say over and over again to myself, racing up the gravel road, rocks spinning under my wheels. "I won't have to leave you for another day, or another week or till summer is over." Then I push open the heavy door with my arms full of groceries, or drop my suitcases on the hooked rug and look at it all over again, as if for the first time. I love every part of it, and it comforts me as only a special place can. The Knob framed in the big window beckons to me like an old friend. "I'll be up there soon," I whisper. "Let me get my boots on first."

Two Miles Down

I T'S A favorite walk of mine: two miles down to my P.O. box on the Haywood County road. Although the road is a good 1,500-foot drop from my house, it's an easy, meandering one, with lots of curves and gentle descents. Going down takes me thirty minutes. Coming back up, a good fifty. I pass my nearest neighbor Jake Moody's cabin, almost at the bottom. I'm glad there's lots of empty land between us. Walking the gravel road is a welcome change from the slippery trails on the property. It rains a lot in the Smokies, daily sometimes, but my roadbed is firm, no roots or holes, and I can keep my eyes on the mountains around me instead of my feet. I can think a lot, too, and reminisce as I walk along.

Enos Boyd, from Jonathan Creek, was our rural mail carrier after we bought the Purchase when the children were young. Over the years Enos became a kind of extended family member from June to September. We left him notes telling him, "Hold the mail, please, we've gone camping." We left him money for stamps, which he kindly put on our letters and left us the change. We left other notes such as "Come up and visit," which he did. At the end of the summer, our last note said "Thanks," attached to a paper plate full of brownies that Suzy, my youngest daughter, made him when we left.

It was Enos Boyd who told us about the chestnut forests at the Purchase. At the bottom of the first part of the road, a quarter mile below the house, is an intersection of roads. We gave it the name of "Five

Points" because our road meets four old grassy logging ones. These abandoned tracks date back to the forties, when the Davey Tree Company contracted for the timber at the Purchase. Near Five Points was what we called a "chestnut graveyard," scattered sawed-off stumps, three to four feet across, testimony to the great forest that stood there once and to the blight that decimated it and all the others from Maine to Mississippi.

"Chestnuts grew all over this part of the country," Enos told us, "and their nuts covered the ground. We boys would walk up here in the fall and gather as many as we could. We couldn't carry nearly enough for everyone who wanted them, so we had to keep coming back. We didn't mind that. We liked hiking up here."

The tree of the pioneers. Find an old cabin anywhere in the Smokies and it'll be built out of twelve- to sixteen-inch-wide chestnut logs, and may even have the original chestnut shingles on the roof. After all these years a few dead trees still stand in my forests, bleached, stripped of their bark, waiting for a winter wind to blow them down. Time has hollowed out the stumps at Five Points. Gone is the rough bark with its furrows, gone the golden brown planes of living wood. Their insides are now a rich mixture of sawdust and leaf mold with miniature gardens of columbine, ferns and cinquefoil. Mosses and lichens creep up their naked butts, clothing them in soft living green.

I like to imagine what my land looked like back then, with giant trees growing everywhere you walked. Folks took them for granted, there were so many of them, an endless supply, and didn't treasure them till they were gone. It took only twenty years for the blight to destroy all of them from the time it was first detected in New York state. A lot of lucky folks ended up with wormy chestnut paneling in their dens. Later Champion Paper came in and cut the dead trees into five-by-five cords for firewood.

Leaving Five Points, the road parallels a small, winding valley. On my right, meadows climb up to the house. On my left, thickets of twelve-foot-high "rose bay" rhododendrons along with hemlocks and maples make an almost impenetrable jungle of tangled forest. When the children were small they played in the dark tunnels under the rhododendrons. Springs bubble up everywhere in here, and streams hatch from them in no time, running aimlessly in and out between the exposed roots. Those years when we loaned the pastures out for cattle, the cows liked the coolness of these glens. Sometimes in there, a cow would spook us, standing silently in the shadows, flicking her tail, escaping the flies out on the meadows.

The "boiling spring" was near here, on the edge of the thicket. My mountain neighbors refer to it this way, giving it a special title for a spring that is no more, except in memory. I've searched the spot where, I'm told, it burst out of the ground, shooting six feet up if you held a pipe over the outlet. Ernest Wood, our first caretaker, told us stories about it. "It made a fine spot for a Sunday picnic," Ernest said. "Ramps grew nearby. We'd dig them up and fry them, have the sweetest water to drink, and let the kids romp about the Purchase."

Further along, the road begins its steady downhill to the mailbox. Off to one side is the old sawmill site. A Christmas tree farm of Fraser firs grows there now. Back in the thirties, though, seven loggers kept two steam engines going with water piped from the "boiling spring." They cut everything big enough to sell. It was Depression time in western Carolina, and timber was one thing there was a lot of. I'm glad I wasn't around to see how the Purchase looked then, stripped of its virgin forests, an ugly sawmill whining all day long as it planed logs into lumber. But Nature is a grand healer. When we bought the land, thirty years later, the forests were back, smaller trees, to be sure, but we hadn't anything to compare them with and they looked beautiful to us.

There was one tree they missed, though. We hadn't had the property more than a few years and I was poking about, exploring where I hadn't been before. In front of me, suddenly, through the weedy stems of laurel and rhododendron, I saw a shadow of something so big, so thick, so dark, I stopped short, staring at it. I pushed my way through the tangle, and there before me was a giant hemlock reaching one hundred feet into the sky. It had to be very old. It had a lightning scar running down its entire length on one side. Maybe that saved it from the saw. Yet it looked healthy, with huge branches of glossy needles. "How could they have missed you?" I said to myself wonderingly. I still remember the thrill of that moment. I hiked back to the house, got my five children together, and had them join hands around it. I didn't have a tape measure. Trying to keep my excitement in check, and hoping I had a champion specimen tree on my hands, I called the Great Smoky Mountains National Park ranger at Cataloochee and asked him to come by and check it out. It turned out I missed having a champion by just a few inches. There were larger hemlocks in the park. But I still show off my tree to tree lovers. It evokes awe in all of them, and in me always a little sadness for a time gone forever when my land was full of trees like it.

I've walked a mile now. Forests of magnolia, maple, and oak arch over the road, keeping it in perpetual shade. Sarvis Gap is off to the left, a pretty little grassy area with a trail up behind leading to Mary's Porch, a knob that juts out over Hemphill, a community of cabins along the county road. Mary's Porch was named for Mary Moody, who lived below it. I guess she hiked up there to get a little peace and quiet. There wasn't a lot to do or many places to go on Sundays for folks living in these mountain coves fifty years ago. They stayed near home. I imagine Mary climbing up to her ledge and eating the blueberries that grow all around it, watching her world down below going about its business. I sit there too, sometimes, and think of her.

Purchase Creek falls off the mountain below Sarvis Gap on its way to Jonathan Creek and Tennessee. It begins at my spring house, bubbling out of a mossy bank and into a tank, from which it is pumped 500 feet up to the house. What we don't use joins up with other waterways and becomes a sturdy stream, crossing under my road through a culvert. After a cloudburst I've seen the force of water rearrange rocks in the streambed, even changing its course slightly, cutting out a bend here or there, or with its collected debris damming a new pool that wasn't there before.

Jake Moody's cabin is around the next bend. I'm almost down now. His hounds will soon be announcing my presence, howling and barking disagreeably and running at me, never recognizing me after all my months of passing by. Only a threatening stance on my part shuts them up. It isn't easy for me to look threatening, but I rather enjoy practicing it when I pass them.

Jake had every right to build this cabin where he did, just off the road on his own land. We owned a joint right-of-way along this part of the road, though he never offered me a penny for keeping it up for him. He built himself a quaint cabin, two stories, with a porch and a stone chimney. He was proud of his handiwork, and well he should be. It sat pretty on the land with the azaleas he'd planted around it to make it look settled. But he was a drinking man and unpredictable. He became wild when liquor got to working on him. Could be sweet and neighborly, putting his arm around my waist, coy-like. A moment later, he could turn mean and threaten to burn my house down. I was careful. When I'd get back each spring and see him outside, I'd blow my horn and wave. I rarely stopped.

One particular day as I walked along, I heard the strangest sucking sound. Jake's dogs hadn't heard my footsteps yet. It was very quiet, no wind. There it was again, a kind of watery "peep, peep," coming out of the soft dirt on the shoulder of the road. I dug at the sound with the toe of my boot. I soon uncovered a garden hose with worn spots that oozed drops of water under the dirt. I walked back up the road, uncovering the hose every so often to make sure it was still there. It led me to one of my year-round springs below Purchase Creek. There, hidden in the weeds, Jake had installed a tiny water tank. Without a word to me he had helped himself to my water. Everyone needs water. I didn't fault him so much for that as for the sneakiness with which he took it. Perhaps I had a little bargaining power now if I ever needed it.

Nothing is perfect. There's a flaw in most things. In beautiful Appalachia the flaw is discarded automobiles. Rarely does any mountain man turn in an old car for a new one. Up here in Hemphill Cove, owners drive them literally into the ground, and that's where they stay. Most are parked just barely off the shoulder of the road, near their cabins, or in unused vegetable patches. Right where they breathed their last. Rusted out, pokeweeds growing up over the seats and out the windows, stripped of tires and propped up on four rocks, they are ugly, useless blights on the landscape.

Jake was accumulating his share of wrecks on the shoulder of our road. An old school bus turned up first. He had great plans for it, living in it, he said, during the summer till he got his house built. Lucky for me he must have tired of it too. One day he pushed it out of sight somewhere down his mountainside. Still, going up to the house, I have to pass a discarded flatbed truck and a beat-up Mercury station-wagon. One day, walking past these wrecks and seeing Jake mowing his lawn, I felt reckless.

"Howdy Jake," I waved. I knew he couldn't hear me over the engine. When he saw me he turned it off and walked slowly toward me up his drive.

"Fine day, isn't it?" I said starting out slow.

"Yep," he said, taking out a cigarette and lighting it.

"Have you got any plans for those old cars of yours on the side of the road?"

"Nope." He was watching me out of the corner of his eye.

"They spoil the looks of the road, Jake. I'm asking you to please get rid of them." There, I got out what I'd meant to say for the last few years.

"You know," he said, looking at me and inhaling a deep breath of smoke, which he exhaled in my direction, "I don't give a goddamn what you want."

I felt the blood rushing to my face in a burst of furious adrenaline. "Jake," I said, keeping my voice even and under control. "I spend a lot of money keeping up the road for you and for me, and you never offer to help me out with it year after year. The road belongs to both of us. I'm asking you to get rid of them."

"Kathy," and he put his face too close to mine for comfort, "I can take the blade of my dozer and tear up my side of the right-of-way and let your part just fall in. Wouldn't take me long to do that. I can get into my land another way, real easy."

Things were getting pretty ugly, and I had to think clearly. I knew a little about rights-of-way. They were legal and binding, ours was here to stay, and no one could deny the other access to his or her property.

"Don't try that, Jake," I said. "The law won't permit it." I walked away from him a bit. "Another thing, how come you tapped my spring without asking? I'd have given the water to you, but you should have asked for it. That's the law too."

Do you think this talk solved anything? I walked away, down to the mailbox that day, seething and trembling. When I came back up the road I tried to walk past Jake's property as fast as I could. He and his dogs had gone inside, thank the Lord.

Well, that crisis is over. The old cars are still there. Jake's still tapping my spring, and I still wave as I go past. The main thing, though, is that he hasn't damaged the road.

There's a lot going on in these woods, a lot of the past and plenty of the present to think about. My faithful *Wall Street Journal* is in my box as usual, plus an LL Bean catalog. No letters. Not a great reward for my four-mile walk. I'll sit on a rock and rest at Purchase Creek on my way back up, and read the paper about what's happening to other folks far away from here.

Mountain Portrait

THAT picture of Leitha and Ernest Wood on my cabin wall could win a prize. My neighbor Dan Matthews took it, and I thank him each time I look at it. It's one of those rare snapshots, a close-up, that's a winner. It's a little faded now after years of mountain sun pouring through the window. Ernest is in his faded bib overalls and wearing an old brown hat, his head cocked to one side, smiling. Leitha, in front, with her straight, short hair tucked behind her ears, hangs her head down a bit, smiling carefully so you can't see her missing teeth, but looking straight at the camera with her clear blue eyes. The whole picture sings of Appalachia, and of love and strength and hardship. Ernest has buried two wives since then and moved off the mountain to Campbell Creek, down in the valley where it's warmer and he can tend his tobacco with both feet on the level.

When my husband and I bought our land, "the Purchase," from Med Leatherwood, he introduced us to Leitha and Ernest. "You won't find better folks than them around here," he said. "If they like you they'll do anything for you." He was right. We hit it off fine from the very start when they came up to share our first dinner by the rock where the house would go. Ernest got the fire going, and we ate the fresh sweet corn and steak I'd brought and got acquainted over some cold beer.

Ernest was part of the team of mountain carpenters who built the house between October and May of that year, 1965. He knew every inch of it, and I guess he marveled with the rest of them at the twenty-foot-high window and "scissors" cross beams that evolved in the big room that faced the Knob. I suppose our vacation house was a conversation piece in that neighborhood of simple, rustic cabins where people lived and worked and raised families.

Leitha and Ernest lived a mile below me, as the crow flies. I could never figure out how old they were. She married Ernest when she was sixteen, she told me. They had raised four sons, hardworking men who built cabins with rock chimneys and played guitars on Saturday nights and told stories you wouldn't believe about their adventures in the mountains. Could be their yarns got better when they had summer visitors like us around to listen. You could tell Ernest had Cherokee blood in him from the shape of his strong, hooked nose. And they were "kin" to about everyone in Hemphill Cove, the mountain community below us, whether by blood or marriage.

They lived in a pretty rock house Ernest had built himself, with a view of Hemphill Bald and a vegetable garden cut into the steep hillside up behind it. He channeled a little spring that trickled off the bank in the front garden and ran it through a hollow log into an enameled basin so Leitha could wash the mud off the cabbage and lettuce after she picked them. I often sat there of an evening, visiting, with the shadows lengthening on the mountains, listening to the spring running in and out of the sink and thinking how peaceful and uncomplicated her life was. They didn't own a car, never had. Their travels were to town, fifteen miles away, and to campgrounds like Big Creek and Cataloochee, where their son, George, took them. They rarely left Haywood County. The world outside was on television, and they could snap it off when they wanted to. They grew about everything they needed and took each day as it came. And they had each other.

I envied them. I wondered what Leitha thought of me rushing up to the mountains in my shiny Jeep, using the house for a few weeks, rushing home to tend to some need two hundred miles away, then back up again with more company, tired and eager for some mountain peace. My husband didn't come up that often, and didn't stay long when he came. He had lots of other interests, and the isolation of the place got to him after a few days. He left it in my hands pretty much.

We had five children, but four of them were about grown up, except for David, who came late in our lives, born ten years after his brother, Peter. The Purchase was truly a second home to these last two children, and a haven to me.

Ernest came up each week to cut the wild mountain grass that grew so fast you could practically see it growing, with all the rain there is in the Smokies. Leitha came with him to help me inside. They washed our big windows with clear water and wiped them dry with newspaper, the best way to make them shine, they said. Ernest vacuumed while Leitha did other things. He even ran my big, heavy Hoover across the couch cushions, till I showed him the attachments were easier to use.

"You'll be needing some shrubbery round the house," he said to me one day after we moved in, as Leitha helped me unpack the dishes. "If you drive the Jeep, I'll show you what we can dig up in the woods."

Off we went, Ernest with his shovel and me in my four-wheel drive. Smoky Mountain woods are filled with rosebay rhododendron and flame azaleas, and in a couple of hours we had all the plants we needed for the corners of the house. I'd never seen root balls so rich with black earth. They went into the holes he'd dug, and today, thirty years later, the rhododendrons are ten feet high and bloom every year.

They always came together, and they always walked. I would have driven down to meet them, but Leitha said, "Lord, Kathy, we need the exercise." I doubted that. They had their special short cuts up the mountain to the Purchase, but it was still two miles each way. They knew the land far better than we did. Med Leatherwood had grazed his cattle there for years, and it had become a playground for all our neighbors who like to hunt and picnic and sit on its hillsides and watch the far-off mountains disappear and reappear.

David was a year old when the house was finished, and Leitha and Ernest took care of him the days they came up to work, so that I could go off hiking in the mountains. I always left written instructions for them about David's schedule: what he ate, when he slept, where the diapers were. "Some scrambled eggs and applesauce for lunch," I wrote, "and wake him up from his afternoon nap by three," and other things I thought they ought to know, like where to find me in an emergency. Off I went, pleased and easy in my mind.

On my return David sat between them on the grassy hillside watching for my Jeep to come around the curve below the house. Whatever had been eaten was cleaned up, whatever had been soiled was washed, dried, and put away. Only months later did I found out neither of them could read a word I wrote. But they know how to keep a baby happy. When my canceled checks came back a month later from the bank, their "mark" was on the back. Banks in the mountains were used to accepting these simple symbols the people used for signatures.

I guess the biggest compliment our family ever received from Ernest and Leitha was when they added on a new room to their cabin. They were mysterious about it for a while. Ernest got his sons to help him but didn't talk much about it. Then one day I went down to pick up some lettuce, and he took me around to the back where the room stood almost finished.

"We call it 'the Purchase room,'" he said. I looked around. There were old chestnut beams across the ceiling and paneling on the walls and a rock fireplace, their first, and a big picture window that looked out at the Bald.

I was touched. "It's beautiful," I said, looking out the new window through the leafy trees to the far-off mountain. I didn't know till then how much they liked what we'd built at the Purchase. Winning their respect meant everything to me.

The years went by and Ernest and Leitha became part of our lives and took care of the Purchase during the long winter months when it was closed up. Winters were hard up there at 5,000 feet; two feet of snow could blow into five-foot drifts and make the road impassable. Mountain people are used to problems and solving them themselves. Isolated as they have been for so many years in mountain coves, and naturally frugal, they learn to fix about anything. If they can't, what won't work sits by the side of the road, discarded, with honeysuckle growing over it till it's covered up.

Leitha and Ernest solved problems at the Purchase when we weren't there and called us later to tell us about them. The phone rang one day in February down home in Southern Pines, where we spent the winters.

"That you, Kathy?" Ernest shouted into the phone. He knew I was a long way off and wanted to be sure I heard him. "Snow's deep up here and still coming. You're out of oil and the pipes'll freeze." He was direct on the phone and always got right down to business.

"Oh, that's terrible," I shouted back. "I'll call the oil man right away." Visions of burst pipes on hardwood floors was a disaster.

"He couldn't get up here," Ernest yelled. "Snow's too deep."

My heart sank. We depended on regular deliveries of oil through the winter months when we weren't there. "What will we do?" I said. I couldn't think of a solution on short notice like this.

"It's all right now," Ernest said, "We took care of it. I thought maybe that heelycopter pilot over at Cataloochee might help us out. But he was gone, so I just hooked up my old mule to a sled, got the oil folks to drop some barrels off as far up the road as they could get, and Bessie and I dragged them the rest of the way. You got plenty of oil now. I even got some extra, just in case."

"Oh, Ernest," was all I could say, "whatever would I do without you?"

The next summer I learned he had made four trips up our road in the snow, dragging the barrels the two miles to the house.

Leitha came extra sometimes to help me out if I had company. She never came empty handed. If it wasn't lettuce from her garden, it was coleslaw or zinnias, the prettiest, biggest zinnias I'd ever seen. We were working together one day, changing sheets. She was fast with beds, quick with anything that needed doing.

"I want you to look at this, Kathy," she said to me that day, un-buttoning her blouse. She had a homemade bandage covering her left breast, and when she pulled it off I saw a raw wound, oozing pus and water.

I was horrified. "Leitha, how long have you had this?"

"It comes and goes. It's better this week," she said, and she buttoned her blouse again.

I was scared for her. I'd never seen anything worse on a person

who kept walking around and not paying any attention to it. "Leitha, let's go see your doctor. I can drive you down the mountain right now."

"Naw, Kathy," she said, "he wouldn't do a thing I'm not already doing. Ernest will take me next week if it gets worse."

I didn't believe she would. She and Ernest were used to taking care of themselves and not relying on outsiders. And I doubted they trusted doctors unless it came down to a matter of life or death. We didn't talk about it again for a while, but I noticed she had a cough now, an intermittent, hacking cough.

Ernest told me one day when we were out in the woods that Leitha had had a "smothering fit" when they were up at the house checking on it that winter. "I just opened the window upstairs and held her outside till she caught her breath." He said it matter-of-factly, as if it didn't worry him a bit. She and Ernest were as close a married couple as I'd ever seen. They were always together working, walking, dancing.

There were dance nights at the Purchase that made the floor shake. All I had to do was put out the word that I wanted to have a party and ask Leitha and Ernest if they'd come and bring the music and show my company how to clog. I supplied cranberry juice for Cal Messer, a violinist from Cosby, who'd sworn off whiskey because he was about blind from bad homemade liquor. I had beer for the rest of Leitha's sons and friends who might turn up. All of them could pick a guitar or a banjo and sing songs till past midnight, until I'd have "to call it" and say we needed rest.

Watching Leitha dance was worth all the trouble. Good cloggers don't move anything but their feet. She was straight as an arrow, swinging just a mite from her waist. It was her feet that moved like lightning, doing a fast shuffle but lightly. Clogging was hard on my oak floor, and after a few clogging evenings we moved out to the garage with its cement floor. That was Ernest's suggestion. He loved the house like I did and was always thinking of ways to care for it.

I didn't think it could ever happen, but one time he and I "fell out." When Leitha walked up alone that day, I knew something was wrong.

"Where's Ernest today?" I asked her.

Leitha looked solemn. "Ernest may have just quit the Purchase," she said.

I couldn't imagine what had happened. My mind raced over our last work day together. Everything had gone as it always went: friendly, busy.

"His feelings are hurt, Kathy." She went over to the sink to clean up after breakfast. "It's the way you said things about his work."

My heart beat fast. I couldn't imagine living there in that lonesome place without his help. "Whatever did I say that hurt him? Tell him I'm sorry. I'd never hurt his feelings for the world."

What had I said, I wondered? I can't remember now exactly what it was, it's so long ago. But it might have been my employer voice demanding instead of asking, friend to friend. Anyway, I remember driving down that very hour and finding him out in his garden. I apologized and told him I couldn't stay at the Purchase without his help. He came back to work, but things were never quite the same. I learned something: You don't tell the mountain people what they're to do for you, you ask them and thank them afterward.

Leitha's cough kept getting worse. It was the next summer after she had shown me her sore. She and Ernest agreed to spend a few nights and chaperone my nineteen-year-old daughter, Gerry, and her boyfriend, who had come to visit while I was away. I turned over my bedroom to them and left a jumbo bottle of cough medicine for Leitha by the bed. It was all gone when I returned, and she claimed it had done her a world of good. Years later, when Gerry had married her boyfriend, the two of them told me with great glee that Leitha and Ernest had gone to bed at eight o'clock each night and left them plenty of time to themselves.

Then that fall I heard from Bonnie, their daughter-in-law, that Leitha was in the hospital in Asheville. I put aside everything and drove up there to see her. The girls took time off from college to go with me. Leitha was propped up in bed with pillows behind her so she could breathe without a coughing fit. Ernest was at her side.

"Don't none of you worry about me," she said, smiling her shy smile. "The doctor's given me some miracle medicine," and she pointed to a bottle of dark syrup on the table. "Ernest is taking me home tomorrow."

I looked at Ernest dubiously. He kept looking at Leitha. He had taken his hat off. I'd never seen him with his hat off before.

She went home just like she said. Two weeks later she was gone. I know now they both knew she was dying and played a game with all of us. She'd had breast cancer for years and lived on in spite of herself, her lungs filling up, making her cough and short of breath.

Ernest buried her in the family cemetery, the prettiest place I'd ever seen for a grave, on top of a little hill not far from his farm in Hemphill. He'd cleared the woods years before and planted purple rhododendrons around the edges, just getting ready, I guess, for when he needed it. Leitha has a stone with her name and dates, and the other half has Ernest's name, his birthdate, and a blank.

Ernest never really worked at the Purchase after that. He came up for visits sometimes, but the old days were gone. He married Nell, a beautician from another county, with blond hair. She loved him and took care of him in her own way. But she became ill too, after a few years, and died. Then he married Lily and moved off the mountain to a trailer in the valley. They were happy for a while, but Lily was diabetic and had lots of health problems. Ernest just knuckled in and did what had to be done. Now he's alone again, keeping busy with a small garden and his tobacco patch. I seldom see him anymore. But I've got my picture of him in happier days.

Bonnie works for me now, and a truer friend I couldn't find. She's as faithful and handy and loving as Leitha was, and the years tick by and Bonnie cares for the Purchase and me and plants my tiny garden with flowers that keep me company all summer long. All I have to do is get there and the house is waiting for me, year after year, clean and cozy. When mountain people like you, you have a double blessing, your mountain home and friends to look after it when you're gone. I'm blessed.

Amos

IN THE southern Appalachians are old, rounded mountains, ridge after ridge after ridge of them, with hollows in between and coves (we call them valleys) where you can live and plant crops, and springs turning up from nowhere and running steady and pure. People call this land the Great Smokies because they're so often misty. But come winter, or after a summer squall, you can see forever, and it's all forests and high, grassy balds just crying out to be climbed.

Our neighbor, Amos Wood, called it home too and showed us trails to walk and where the trout hung out and generally kept me and my children company during the summers, roaring up the mountain at odd times on his Honda. I was alone a lot with my five children. Amos' visits were welcome to us. He was in his thirties when I first met him, maybe ten years younger than I. Homely, with a prominent hook nose he inherited from his Cherokee father and a red weathered face to go with his red hair, he was pleasing and cheerful, and we became friends right off. A true woodsman, he could read signs in the way the grass was bent or the branch broken. He also know where the Catawba rhododendron bloomed and where to find ginseng.

Our properties adjoined the Great Smoky Mountains National Park, and I expect a good deal of Amos' time was spent dodging the rangers who were searching for poachers or mountain folk fishing out of season. A lot of people were unhappy when the government took over hundreds of miles of their hunting land and made a national park of it sixty years ago.

A lot of old habits had to change. If your quarry was a deer or a bear who was smart enough to run away to safety onto federal land, you had to let it go. Rules were broken in the beginning, still are, and park rangers are few and widely spaced. Amos knew those woods and laurel slicks like his own backyard. I saw him pass my kitchen window one evening early, years back, carrying a pillowcase full of something he'd dug up in the park, I guess. I hollered at him to stop awhile and chat, but he was in a hurry that time. He may have been digging "sang" or, more probably, "ramps," wild onions, the locals call it.

"Sang," for ginseng, is a rather inconspicuous plant with a man-like root system, much prized in China as an aphrodisiac. Big sums are paid for it still, and the quality in the Appalachians is especially fine. But picking it in the park is as illegal as making moonshine. In bygone years, before the park, mountain families added to their incomes picking "sang."

Amos knew our land well. After all, our boundaries touched, and he had used it like his own before we came. Ours was a tract of 550 acres that had lain empty for years except for the cattle that grazed on its high meadows. When we turned up as new owners it didn't seem to daunt the neighborhood at all. People around there continued walking all over it, not hunting anymore, at least not while we were there, but driving their girlfriends or mothers up to see the view and the new house or chat with me over the cold beer I kept on hand. I learned mountain ways fast, and it brought me luck and good friends. I never turned anyone off my place, invited or not. What would be the use of that? They'd be back the minute summer was over and my Jeep going around the last curve to where the county road began. Might as well let them enjoy it and thank me for my hospitality. There was an old log cabin on the place. I never locked it but left it clean and open, hoping its visitors would keep it so. Most times they did, and left my house on the mountain above alone.

Amos was a teller of tall tales. He talked like he was quoting God's Truth, though you knew in your heart he was kidding. "Hollow logs are fine places to sleep in," he told us once. "Just shoo the other critters out that were in there first." I pretended to be astounded at his stories, and that suited him fine and spurred him on to tell wilder ones until it grew late and I had to ask him to supper. He rarely stayed to eat—part of mountain caution, I decided. Maybe he thought I'd poison him or enchant him with my herbs. He enchanted all of us instead for twenty years.

He had a way with the ladies. He never married. I expect he had too much fun romancing other men's wives. Why he never got his share of buckshot from his neighbors, I'll never know. Every few years a girlfriend would move in with him and he'd act happy and kind of settle down for a time, and then she'd drift on. One of these was a graduate of Wellesley College who had come to North Carolina to study the Appalachian dialect. She certainly picked the right place for that. She and Amos acted crazy about each other, and she filled her notebooks up easily with Amos' crowd hanging around. In time she drifted along, like all the others.

I had my own trouble along that line. After twenty-eight years of marriage, I decided to leave my husband. We had been traveling in separate directions for years. I had driven to the house alone early one spring day to collect myself and do some sad reckoning on the future. I ran into Amos on his motorcycle as I drove up my road. I'll never forget the conversation we had that day. He had an intent way of really listening to you, as though he cared a lot about what you said. Then he'd make some kind of wise summing-up comment that let you know he understood it all.

"Alone, Kathy?" he asked me, looking at the empty car.

I confessed to him that I was depressed and had driven up for a few days by myself to inhale some good mountain air.

"You'll be all right here after a spell. Came to the right place, Kathy." If he saw a tear or a trembling lip, he didn't let on.

"What's ever wrong gets right here," he continued. "Just you sit on that porch of yours and look at the mountains. They never change, not like people. You can always trust them. Oh, they may hide once in a while, get clouded up, but they always come back out. It's like finding old friends again. You'll see," he promised. He gunned up his bike, and waved, and went on down the road.

He was right. I mended in time, couldn't help it with all that beauty around me. And Amos came up a lot that summer, to cheer me up, I guess. We went fishing with my boys and he showed us the hang of stealing up on a trout without our shadows spooking it first. Sometimes we'd just sit, all of us, or maybe just Amos and me, out on the porch, our feet propped up on the railing, watching the lights come on in the valley below and the sunset colors slowly fading away into darkness. I felt a certain peace pushing out the sadness in my heart.

I had a lot of house guests in the summertime, and they were all intrigued by Amos. Most of them were awed by the isolation I lived in and the 5,000-foot mountains all around them. Amos' way of talking and looking completed the picture for them. They knew then they had stepped into another world. They didn't always understand his vocabulary and that "whupped" meant "whipped," and "fur piece" a goodly distance. But after these small hurdles they sat back and laughed and asked for more. Amos was always respectful to my guests, but he loved having an audience.

"We've got to expose these folks to our ways, Kathy," he'd say in front of them. "How'd you all like to go on a bear hunt?" he asked them one day. "They'd like that," he said, turning to me all serious.

My guests always bit on that one. "You didn't tell us you had bears up here," they said uneasily. "How often do you see one?"

"Rarely. Almost never," I said positively. I decided to change the subject.

Amos made a party. He played the guitar and sang, but after a while he just had to get up and dance. Could he clog! When he did that shuffling mountain jig step, he never moved his upper body at all; his legs flew about loose and limber as if they were on strings and someone else was pulling them. He was a sight to see, clogging to a fast fiddle. He was something to listen to, too, when he played his guitar and sang songs I'd never heard and some I had. Saturday nights he and his friends played music and drank, sang some more and drank some more. Weekends after long work weeks were their rewards, and partying lasted all night. I never saw Amos drunk. I knew when to leave those fiddling parties, and when they came to play at my house, they knew when to leave, too. They treated me differently. Carefully, is a better way to put it. I was an outsider, after all.

His devotion to beer was graphically evident one night when he

startled my guests awake by phoning me after midnight.

"I'm out of beer, Kathy," was all he said.

"That's too bad, Amos," I said. I had no doubt who he was. "But it's midnight and I was asleep."

"But we're out of beer," he repeated. "If you'll just put a six-pack out on the porch railing by the kitchen we'll come up and not bother you a bit." He assumed I always had a supply of beer.

"Surely you're not going to give him beer at this hour?" my friends asked in disbelief. Six of them were leaning over the stairs in their nightgowns, staring down at me as I hung up the phone. "Does this kind of thing go on very often up here?"

"Not too often," I said, taking the beer from the refrigerator and going out on the porch. I knew it wouldn't be long before he turned up, and I wanted the house dark again and not "inviting-in" looking. My friend decided to sit up in the dark with me and watch for the next act. Before long, up my winding road two headlights appeared. They eased into the yard over the grass very quietly as we watched from inside. The Jeep neared the porch railing, and a hand reached out and neatly picked up the beer without stopping. Suddenly, we heard a crunch of wood. I knew what had happened. They had run over the steps. If they heard it, they never stopped. They slipped away as quietly as they had come, down the road, never stopping. The next morning I surveyed my steps. They would need replacing. Later Amos called to thank me for the beer. I told him he owed me new steps. He came up shortly and fixed them, over a can of beer, chatting with my guests as they hung around him, watching him replace the lower step with a new plank he had brought along. I could see his charm working on them. They would most likely supply him beer at midnight too, sometime, if he asked them.

Amos kept promising me a purple rhododendron, the wild kind that grew in certain hard-to-reach places in the Smokies. He had an affection for growing things that I understood, liking them especially too. I never got the rhododendron, but one time when I returned after months away, I noticed a bush at the corner of the porch where none had been before. I was mystified, wondering where it had come from, what it was, and who had planted it. It had pretty white flowers with a strong, sweet perfume. Then I thought of Amos.

"It's a wild mock orange," he said. "The house needed something there."

He could never grow old, but the last few years of his life he kind of settled down. After he went on a wild driving spree, the State Patrol assigned him to "community service" at a local nursing home. He soon won his way into the old hearts there, too, and had a steady girl, a nurse, Carolyn, who worked there and loved him now. But he wasn't to live much longer. When he was fifty-four he was stricken with a brain tumor which took six months to carry him off. His father, Ernest, said it was from an old injury when he was pushed or fell off the back of a moving truck. He suffered terrible head pains, and the tumor affected his talking and movement. A week before he died I went to visit him. He smiled at me as I held his hand. I told him of all the things that reminded me of him. I told him that the mountains had "brought me around," just like he had predicted they would. He pressed my hand. I told him I had more friends coming that wanted him to teach them how to clog. He shook his head and smiled as best he could. I didn't stay long. He had his whole family around him now, just waiting and talking quietly.

His funeral was at the graveside, his coffin covered with wildflowers and creeping cedar and a touch of 'seng picked by many of his friends early that morning. He's buried in a tiny mountain cemetery, where his mother lies, and the purple rhododendrons make a circle about their graves.

Neighbors

THE CABIN was right below my mailbox on the county road, and I passed it every day in the summertime when I went up or down the mountain. For as long as I can remember it had been empty. It was a sight, even for Appalachia. Rags were stuffed in the openings where windows had once been. The porch was packed with old lumber and broken-down furniture. The yard was scattered with bits of car parts and junk. A Maytag washer sat under a tree, rusted out, and nosed into the bank above the house was an abandoned pickup truck, its wheels removed long ago, propped up on four rocks.

My neighborhood, Hemphill, North Carolina, was one place in the USA where "trade-ins" ended up on the shoulder of the road, driven till the last gasp of life left them and they were abandoned to become part of the scenery. I got used to these wrecks I'd pass going up to my place, and I tried to keep my mind on the blue mountains surrounding me instead.

One spring, not so far back, driving up the mountain in my Jeep, loaded with groceries and belongings for my annual summer vacation, I passed the cabin and noticed a line of wash running from the porch to a tree, and a little curl of smoke coming out of the stovepipe at the side. I asked Bonnie about it when she came to help me move in. Bonnie and her husband, George, were my friends and caretakers. They lived there and knew everything that happened in Hemphill Cove, North Carolina, this seven-mile stretch of road with small cabins and farms running alongside it and, behind them, Hemphill Creek, pouring down off the mountain from higher up.

"That cabin belongs to Jamie Sutton. He's back home, out of prison," she said, unpacking the groceries and putting them on the shelf. "Served his time, I reckon. I sure hope he goes straight for a change. Trouble with Jamie is the company he keeps. Otherwise he's a good sort. George has got him a job at the sawmill."

"Bonnie, how many people has George brought to the sawmill over the years?" I could count six at least, half of them his relatives. George was kind, always helping a person get back on his feet.

"Jamie's all alone now," she continued, pressing the paper bags flat and putting them away in the closet. "You might have heard some years back how he found his daddy dead under a tractor, bled to death, mowing too steep a side of the pasture. It turned over on him. That was a terrible day for Jamie."

I shivered, imaging the scene. Mountain people took lots of chances, farming on steep land, needing to make the most of what was theirs. I felt sad for Jamie.

Each time I passed his cabin now, I noticed different things. He had a red chow dog that he kept on a long chain while he was at work. The yard stayed exactly the same, littered, and the cabin too; but when he was at home, no matter the temperature, the door stood open. He had placed a straight-back chair, like one out of a dining room set, on the side of the road by his mailbox. It looked very strange there, very proper, as though its owner planned to have a front seat at some event about to happen on the road.

One day I slowed down when I got to his place, just looking to see if there was anything different. It was Saturday, and the door was open. I saw Jamie in the yard. He was naked to the waist, though it was nearly June and cool. He waved, and I waved back. On an impulse (I'm old now, but I still follow impulses, and he was my neighbor after all) I stopped and rolled down the window.

"Good morning," I yelled.

"Morning," he said, putting down the wrench he was using.

I couldn't think of anything suitable to say. "Pretty day, isn't it?"

"Yep. Mighty pretty day."

I put the car in gear again and slowly moved on. But I felt better.

It was good to slow down and not rush past, as I did so often, past these simple little cabins, too busy with my own affairs, eager to reach my own comfortable place and my well-fed friends who were waiting for my return.

The next time Bonnie came, I told her I'd met Jamie at last. She was helping me fold the sheets.

"George says Jamie never brings any lunch to work. Between them at the mill they split up their food and make enough for him. He tells them he's not hungry, but they give it to him anyway. It's a long time between six in the morning when they arrive and six at night when they go home." She shook her head. "There's not much extry to eat around Jamie's, either, he got so many debts to pay. The power people turned off his electricity several times because he didn't pay his bill," she continued. "That didn't stop Jamie. He just took a meter off someone's cabin who was gone and hooked it up to his wall. After a while they found out and slapped another fine on him. I think he's got power now."

I thought he sounded mighty ingenious. "Is he a good worker at the sawmill?" I asked.

"George says he's steady, doesn't come drunk either. Of course the mill wouldn't keep no one a minute if he acted the least bit drunk. Jamie knows that, and he's careful, weekdays anyways."

I was getting a picture of my neighbor.

The weeks went by and I settled in. It was late June now, and the flame azalea along the banks above the road was blooming in all shades of orange. About the prettiest sight one could see. Hanging over Jamie's old pickup truck was an especially pretty azalea, and I slowed down to admire it. I saw Jamie bending over a motorcycle, working on the engine, bare to the waist as usual. He straightened up and waved. My window was down. The weather was getting warm.

"It's such a pretty color," I yelled to him, pointing to the bush. Then I pulled over by his mailbox, where the wooden chair sat. He walked over slowly.

"I'm Kathryn McNeil. It's good to see your cabin open again." We shook hands through the window. He had the bluest eyes I'd seen for a while. He looked thirtyish, though his skin was red and rough from years of exposure and other things I could only guess at. His long red hair was tied back with a rag, and it, and his ruddiness, gave him a kind of tawny look.

"Who sits in the chair?" I asked.

"I do," he sat down in it and crossed his legs.

It was a silly question. He looked at home in it. After all, it was his chair.

"George picks me up each morning, and I just sit here and wait."

How odd, I thought, to be sitting here in the dark at six in the morning, just waiting. But at least he was ready and not keeping anybody waiting, which was more than I could say for others I knew.

"Best be on my way, I guess," I said, smiling at him. "I'm interfering with your repairs there," and I started my engine.

"Don't matter a bit," he said, sitting there still in his chair, swinging his crossed leg and looking at me.

"See you soon." I waved again and drove up the road.

I asked Bonnie the next time she came to work if Jamie would be insulted if I left him some extra food. There is always that fine line with working people living on the ragged edge. I certainly didn't want to hurt his feelings. Bonnie reassured me he'd be pleased. One day while he was at work, I left half of a roasted chicken and some cooked yams in a brown bag in the yard. When I approached, the chow dog growled at me. I backed off and looked for someplace near the porch but off the ground. There was an old stump with hubcaps piled on it. I dumped the hubcaps on the ground and put the bag there instead and wrote "Jamie" and my initials on it. I hoped no animal would get to it during all those hours it would sit there. The next day when I made my trip down the mountain, I looked to see if a dog had scattered the bag around the place, but I saw no signs. Jamie must have found it. Now I knew where to take my leftover food this summer.

Almost every week I left a bag on the stump, and it was always gone when I drove by the next day. Once I left a casserole. Eventually I got the dish back. Jamie gave it to George, who gave it to Bonnie, who brought it back the next Wednesday when she came to work. Meanwhile, we kept waving to each other, Jamie and I, when I passed him on weekends. That was the extent of our connection until one Sunday afternoon when I had "callers."

I was lying in the hammock out on the back lawn, half reading, half watching the clouds move across the mountains, when I heard a loud banging on the front door. Startled, I walked inside and peeped out the window near the front door. Jamie and another man were standing there. Jamie was dressed neatly, but his companion was a stranger to me and was shirtless and groggy looking. Against my better instincts I opened the door.

"Mrs. McNeil, I've come to thank you," Jamie said. "This here's my friend Bud."

His friend wavered and looked like he might be ill. I was caught at a loss. Should I visit with them outside, or invite them in? Would I get them out once they came in? Jamie looked friendly, and his eyes seemed bluer than ever in his red face. I held the door open.

Jamie strolled inside, looking at the beams in the high ceiling, the soft couches by the fireplace, the general roominess around him. His friend staggered as he followed him to the table in the window, where

I usually sat with visitors. The view was nice from there.

"The lady wants you to sit here, Bud," Jamie said roughly to his friend, pushing him down into a chair.

I knew I had a problem. I could now see that Bud was dead drunk. He might get sick any minute. My mind switched back and forth from how to get rid of them politely, to what I might grab to give Bud if he needed help in a hurry. His head had fallen on his chest.

What a fool I was to get caught all alone, inside, with a couple of unpredictable mountain men. I looked at Jamie. He was looking around the room admiringly, at the wall hangings from Ecuador, at the watercolors of the mountains on the walls, at the stereo on the bookshelf.

"How's your work going at the sawmill?" I asked him, trying to get a handle on my nerves.

"Just dandy," Jamie answered. He was slouched in his chair and didn't look like he would be moving any time soon.

It crossed my mind that I might be robbed by these two. Why not? I had so much, and they had nothing. I had asked for it, stepping into this forlorn man's life with my offerings of food and bits of neighborliness.

Bud groaned and, opening his eyes, looked at me vaguely and belched. I don't know which bothered me more at that moment, the fear of being robbed or the fear of him becoming ill inside my house. I think the latter.

Jamie leaned over and cuffed him roughly on the side of his head.

"Shut up, you fool," he said fiercely to him. "You're in the presence of a lady."

Bud groaned again and put his arm up defensively, shielding his face from another blow.

I knew then and there I was safe. Jamie wouldn't hurt me.

"I think you both better go now," I said smiling faintly at Jamie. I stood up and placed my chair carefully under the table, hoping to encourage them to stand, too.

"Bud's not well," I continued, "and I don't want him here. I know you understand, Jamie." I hoped I might appeal to his sense of fitness, if such existed for him.

He stood too, after a moment. "We'll go now, Mrs. McNeil. Just wanted you to know I'm grateful for the food." They walked to the door with me, Jamie weaving a little too, I thought. Opening the door, Jamie gave Bud a mighty shove and pushed him out. He hit the side of the house and slowly slumped to the concrete patio, blood dripping down his face from an ugly cut where his face had hit the wall.

I stood there dumbfounded. Then, without a word, Jamie dragged him to his feet, and half-carrying, half-pushing him, got him into the truck they'd come in. Down the road they went and disappeared out of my sight around a curve. I continued to stand there, watching, wanting to be sure they'd keep going. I saw the truck emerge from the woods for a few seconds and disappear again around another curve. I was alone again.

The soft mountain breeze picked up and beckoned me up the hill and into the woods. I needed to walk, to think, to shed the brutality I had so recently been part of. I had glimpsed another world far away from mine, yet almost next door.

I went away shortly after this and didn't return for several weeks. When I drove up the road, Jamie's cabin looked locked up and the chow dog was gone.

"Where's Jamie?" I asked Bonnie when she came up on her weekly visit.

She shook her head and sat down with me at the table in the window to have a cup of coffee before she started her work.

"He's back in jail," she said. "Sheriff came to the sawmill and took him away last week. Seems like he got involved in one of those insurance scams. A friend of his asked him to drive his new truck and wreck it for the insurance. I guess he's lucky he didn't get killed."

We sipped coffee silently together, looking at the mountains. What was there to say? Just beyond the porch the blue ridges stretched, one after one, as far as the eye could see.

Summer Encounters

HIGH up in the Great Smoky Mountains of North Carolina that straddle the border between North Carolina and Tenessee is black bear country. It's land that's full of blueberries and wild apple trees from old farms that have vanished with the years. I spend three months of summer there at my cabin on property known as the Purchase, right on the Cataloochee Divide, a ten-mile ridge running between Polls Gap and Cove Creek. My neighbor, Great Smoky Mountains National Park, owns all the land west of the ridge, and its boundary line is an old chestnut rail fence running down the spine. Built by the CCC "boys" in the Depression, the fence still stands and divides my land from the park.

Fall is hunting season, and bears are smart around here and know they're safe inside the park. Hunts go through the night whenever the moon is full and the hounds need exercise. It's mostly for coon or possum, though; bear hunting is a bigger project. It's a lonesome sound, that faraway baying of the hounds. I lie in bed listening, thinking about the little animal that's climbed high up in a tree trying to escape.

Hounds get lost sometimes, and the morning after a hunt can wander back to my place and lie around eyeing the water faucet. I fill a bucket for them then. The phone rings after a while and a voice says, "You seen my hound dog there at the Purchase? He's got a black spot on his right leg."

"Come and get him," I'll answer. "He's resting. I don't expect he'll go far today."

Ernest, my caretaker of many years, who lives below the Purchase in Hemphill Cove, knocked at my door late one October evening when I was up for a weekend.

"We've tracked a bear close by, Kathy, right above the spring-house." He sounded excited for someone who's been hunting for sixty years. Bears do that to folks.

"I don't want any bears killed on the Purchase, Ernest." I love wild things, though I know bear meat can feed a family for a week. What happens when I'm not here, I ask myself? Plenty. I know better than to tack "No Hunting" signs up on trees. They'd just make good target practice for my neighbors.

The Great Smokies are about the oldest mountains anywhere. "Great" means venerable here in southern Appalachia. Their peaks, worn down by the ages, have become rounded and comfortable. You can live on top of them. Rich hardwood forests cover their slopes. Climb to 6,000 feet and balsam and spruce take over the ridges. The mountain "coves," valleys, are wonderlands of tulip poplar, silverbell, and magnolia, to name a few, growing to specimen size in the heavy rainfall. And "balds," bare mountaintops covered with heath instead of trees, are scattered in between. Everyone has his own favorite bald to visit in June. Then they're brilliant with the colors of purple, pink, and flame from the rhododendron, laurel, and wild azalea that cover them.

It's pretty land, the Purchase, with its high, sunny meadows where you can sit and see forever. I never named it that; it was on the deed and named long ago for someone who might have meant "Perches" for the little mountain on the place with its rocky topknot, or "Purchase" because it meant a lot to someone a hundred years back who bought it and planted potatoes in its black soil and drank deep from its running springs. An old cabin sits beside my spring. Built of chestnut logs fifteen inches wide, it has a rock chimney whose fires have warmed many a hiker caught in an Appalachian downpour. Against the advice of my mountain neighbors who live year around, I built my house five hundred feet above my spring and pump the water uphill. "To see the view," I explained to them.

"It's warmer down in the holler," they said, shaking their heads.

But I notice when they come to visit, they like to sit on my porch and look out at the mountains.

Mt. Pisgah and Cold Mountain are straight ahead, fifty miles away, clear as a bell in October. I feel like I'm level with some of them. I can see into Tennessee from my porch, and Interstate 40 below me looks like a white snake following the Pidgeon River to Knoxville. Can't hear it, that's the best part. Early morning is the best time for looking. The sky is matchless then, not a cloud. As the sun climbs, it draws the moisture out of the heavy forest, and by eleven o'clock the weather has changed. It might rain. Back will go all that water in the clouds, back to the forest. Sit out the rain for an hour or two and you may see forever again, ridge after ridge, unfolding in front of you, as the mist lifts from this one and then that. That's where the term "Smoky" comes from.

Before I opened the cabin one year, Ernest phoned me in eastern Carolina, where I spend my winters. It had to be something serious for Ernest to call.

"A bear's tore out your screen door," he shouted. "Had to be something big," he yelled. "I got the screen fixed, though he may be back."

I hung up the phone. I was excited too. My place was still wild, I thought, despite all the comforts I'd brought to it. I was eager to return.

A week passed, and Ernest was on the phone again.

"He's done it again," he shouted, his voice a mixture of disbelief and admiration. "Ripped it clean off the frame. We're going to catch him this time. Amos is going to camp all night on the porch. Going to leave a trail of tuna fish from the dump to the house."

That was going to be a lot of tuna cans, I thought. My compost dump was a good two hundred yards away.

"No shooting, Ernest. Scare him off. Okay?"

Futile words. I knew it as I heard myself say them. Ernest's son, Amos, was disappointed. He waited out three nights and didn't see a thing. A month later it was my turn. I was back for the summer and lying in bed about 5:30 A.M. watching dawn deepen in the east, wondering what I'd do that day. Suddenly I heard a terrible clawing and tearing of metal. I sat bolt upright in bed, my heart pounding away. That bear was coming in for coffee, I thought, and I'd better be out of there fast! I jumped up and grabbed my robe. But I had to peep just once around the corner at the glass door. There, in the early light, clawing away at the screen, was the biggest raven I'd ever seen. He stood two feet tall at least. He deserved that poem written about him. He spied me in my white nightgown and took off in a fright. I had to laugh. The men were disgusted when I told them, wasting all that time on a bird.

Leitha, Ernest's wife, summed it up best. "I've been thinking, Kathy," she said, her blue eyes wise and clear in her sunburnt face, "That bird was sex-starved, seeing his reflection in the glass."

We'll never know. She might have been right.

I forgot about bears after that. I walked my trails summer after summer, checking on important things like did I have as many Turk's-cap lilies as last year, and would the berry crop be a bumper one? Sometimes I'd come to a grassy place, off by itself with highbush blueberries hanging over it and the grass all matted down like someone had spent a cozy night, and I'd wonder. Bear or deer? I've plenty of deer, and grouse. And foxes. For two weeks, a pair of silver foxes did a dance on my lawn every night between eight and nine o'clock, just before dark. I expect they felt safe then. They'd leap about like puppies, then stop and snoop in the grass after something I couldn't see, then up in the air they'd go again. Just glad to be alive. I began to depend on their visits. I even invited friends up for dinner to see the show. Just as suddenly, they stopped coming. I hoped the baying of the hounds I heard one night hadn't changed things for them.

Animal scat tells you something about who your neighbors are. One morning last summer I was on my way to the compost heap when I passed a steaming clump of scat, six inches wide and purple with half-digested berries. I'd never seen bear scat before, but I knew what it was immediately. It was so fresh I spun around expecting to see him looking at me from behind a tree. Sounds crazy, I know, but I began to sing. I never sing anymore, but words just peeled out of me from long-forgotten ditties learned decades before when I was a Scout leader. I trilled away as I walked back to the house, faster than usual.

The year before had been a bad time for wildlife. Food was scarce, and bears had gone into hibernation hungry. A month ago a woman over on Lost Ridge was trapped in her home for three hours while two bears hung around eating up all her Purina dog food in the shed.

"Bears won't hurt you, Kathy," Ernest chided me. "They scare awful easy. Just don't get between a mother and her cubs. That's when they turn mean."

"Just how am I supposed to know where her cubs are, Ernest, if I can't see them?"

Bear scat increased. I found piles all over the property, never any near the house, though. I guess I was meant to sing my way as I walked this summer. I even looked up an old song book so I wouldn't get bored with myself. I certainly wanted any bear to hear me in advance.

There's a back way to the old cabin by the springhouse. It weaves down an abandoned logging road with mountain laurel arching over it, making a green tunnel for me to walk through. Springs are born along here, and several of them together make a passable creek by the time they reach the cabin.

Springs are vibrant things, rainwater trickling underground, following mysterious, subterranean passageways, down, down, to surface on my land or someone else's. Arbitrary. Capricious. Never disturb the mouth of a spring, I was told. Today was a day to replenish springs. It had rained maybe two inches by noon. It stopped at last, and a cold, soupy fog took its place.

I had company staying with me who chafed to get outside and have some exercise. The temperature had dropped to the forties. Dressed in boots and parkas, we walked to the cabin. Visibility was zero in the thick fog, but there was excitement in seeing a familiar world become strange and shadowy. It was rhododendron time, and ten-foot-high bushes of them grew on either side of the trail, looming above us in the wet gloom, their flowers like soft, luminous globes lighting our way. We tripped, we slipped, we laughed. Then the hiker in the lead held up his hand, his finger on his lips. Ahead in the fog a bear poked about in the streambed, turning over rocks while her cubs scampered about, mimicking her. We watched them silently, then, without a word, in unison, we began to back up, one by one, until we could turn around and climb back to the house. My guests were elated as they shed their dripping gear, and spent the rest of the evening telling bear stories to each other.

•

It was the end of August and time to leave. Monardas in the meadows were all shades of lavender. I'd pick a bouquet, put it in a vase, go out again and find more in a darker lavender and pick them, too. Ernest said my big room looked like a funeral parlor with all the flowers about. Each armful I picked seemed to capture a moment outside and make it last a little longer. I hated to leave. Even the act of hanging the quilts on the clothesline to air before storing them away seemed like a benediction, with mountains looking their grandest all around and the air soft and warm. I had one last guest. She and I would close the house and head east, out of the mountains, back to city streets and houses in rows. We sat at the round table in the corner window, eating dinner by candlelight with the stereo softly playing in the background.

"You didn't tell me you had a dog," my friend, Rhoda, said all of a sudden, rather reproachfully it seemed, staring out at the night behind me.

I looked at her in surprise. "Rhoda, you know I don't have a dog. You've been here three days," I added pointedly.

"What's that, then?" she said, pointing out the window.

I turned around and saw a bear, his nose against the glass, the candlelight shining in his eyes. He had put his paws up on the windowsill so he could look in at us and see what we were eating. We eyed each other with a quarter inch of insulated glass separating us. He didn't move, nor did we, for a full minute. Not a twitch.

"Look at him," I breathed the words, not moving a muscle, "right on the porch." It was as if my whole summer was there in that big, solid body. All the wildness and beauty that shared the land with me, unseen mostly, but there nevertheless. Four more seconds and he was gone, hopping over the porch railing, leaving not a trace of his visit. I rushed outside to catch a last look, but the night had swallowed him.

"Goodbye," I whispered. There was nothing else out there in the darkness except the black shapes of the mountains and a few faraway lights, high up on their sides, of other homeowners, like me maybe, picking lonesome ridges to live on, fitting in, savoring the land.

Max Patch

T WAS the first week of May, and I was back in my cabin again in the southern Appalachians for another spring and summer. "May's too late," my Asheville, North Carolina, friends told me time and time again. "Come in April if you really want to see spring come to the Smokies." My friends don't live at 5,000 feet. In April the world's still asleep at my place. The forest is cold and empty, buds tight and snug on their twigs, meadows still bleached from winter frosts. Botanists will tell you that every 1,000 feet in elevation delays spring by a week.

There is always a fear among wildflower enthusiasts like myself that one might have picked the wrong week to come, maybe one week too early or one week too late. That I might miss the one most exquisite flower of all and have to hear about it from others. One always misses something, I told myself. I had poured over my books all winter, studying the flowers and their pictures, honing my memory so that I would know the structure of nodding Mandarin, or twisted stalk, on sight.

I live in two worlds now. Eight winter months in San Francisco, four summer ones at the Purchase. Dividing the year this way suits me just fine. Along about March, though, I feel like I'm changing gears inside. Nothing outwardly perceptible, just little things: a pile of books for hammock reading begins accumulating in the corner of the closet next to new, waterproof boots. Calls to North Carolina show up frequently now on my phone bill. The leak in the chimney has gotten worse, I'm told. Not to worry, I tell myself, I'll be there soon.

•

After an eight month's absence, I drive up the old familiar road one late afternoon. Anticipation still wells up inside, even after thirty years, with the hope that nothing will have changed. There is a change. The large white oak at the spring has fallen and lies stretched out across the tiny watercourse. I slow down and stop, grieving for it, wondering what month it fell. It looks undignified lying there, its massive trunk sticking up in the air, branches broken and scattered about the meadow. More slowly now, I drive up the last stretch to see my house again, unchanged, its rafters casting the old beloved shadows over the wide porch, lonely and waiting for me on its little mountain.

I lie in bed this first morning and watch the glow of sunrise flush the eastern sky. Slowly, ridges and peaks present themselves, rising out of the cold dawn light like old friends, shaping up in their familiar forms. Pisgah straight ahead on a line with my window, a perfect mountain, pointed and even. Cold Mountain on Pisgah's right, dark and gloomy, its black-forested shoulders spread out with many summits. A complicated mountain. And Max Patch fifty miles away to the north. I have to sit up straight in bed to see it. Its grassy summit looks brassy in the early light. I have a date this week to climb Max Patch with my neighbor Jane Alexander.

Jane is in that very special category called "summer friends," friends one returns to after months of separation, picking up right where we left off last September when we said goodbye. We have the same priorities, Jane and I. Wildflowers and dry weather take precedence over everything else. If the phone rings early and the day is fine, it's pretty sure to be Jane. We will walk seven miles on the Appalachian Trail to Lemon Gap, where we'll have left a car. The trail winds its way for 2,000 miles, crossing the top of Max Patch and descending into the forest below on its way from Georgia to Maine. In May this stretch of the trail is wildflower country without peer.

If ever there was a name that speaks of Appalachia, it would be Max Patch. Max, I guess, owned a patch of mountain 4,500 feet high. That's high for these parts. Its name brings it down to homey size, reduces it to Max's pasture, where he ran his cattle summers when the grasses grew high. These mountains are full of cozy words that turn a mountain pass into a "gap," a valley into a "cove," a peak into a "knob." Low land might be called "bottoms," and high land "tops." It's logical. Names like "Charlie's Bunion" and "Pretty Hollow Gap" tamed the wilderness a hundred years ago for folks whose cabins nestled right in the immensity of it all. It hovered there, just beyond their chestnut fences.

So there we were, Jane and I, together again, climbing the log steps to the top of Max Patch on a blue sky morning made for the gods. Purple violets led us skyward along with "self heal," a mint that loves warm meadows. Max Patch is a bald, a treeless summit, a phenomenon of the Smoky Mountains. No one knows why trees shun these open mountaintops. Most are covered with heaths: rhododendron, mountain laurel, and wild azaleas. There have been decades of speculation about the balds: Did Indians burn them off to keep the forest away? Is there a quality of the soil that discourages hardwoods and conifers? Whatever the reason, this grassy bald gave us a grand view. Nothing small and intimate about it. No farmhouses or steeples in sight, just space and hundreds of miles of blue mountains in every direction. Ridges and knobs, coves and balds, and hawks gliding above us on invisible currents of their own. We sat down to rest in the deep grass.

I looked through my binoculars, trying to figure out where we were and where we had come from. Purchase Knob, the little mountain on my farm, was lost in the endless panorama before us. There's restoration of the spirit in such a view. All the problems of life are put in perspective by the grandeur of the scene. I felt as if a hole had been drilled into my brain, letting in fresh, cold air, flooding out any gnawing worries that lay beneath the surface. We were lost in our own thoughts sitting there.

"We've got a ways to go," Jane said, standing up at last. Jane keeps us on schedule. She knows how long it takes to hike seven miles. And, what's more, she has a husband waiting for her at home. Lucky Jane. I remember the feeling.

We crossed the long summit of Max Patch and descended to the forest below. No shade in these woods yet. Indeed, it was the presence of sunlight into the awakening, still leafless, forest that presented us with what we had hoped to see. Maple flowers spilled out of their opening buds. The serviceberry tree, with its angular white petals, drooped over our heads. New leaves on the hickories uncurled as we watched. And on the ground were thousands of spring beauties, flower faces of tiny pink cups with veins of magenta. Mingled with them were the fine-cut gray leaves of Dutchman's breeches, white pantaloon shapes hanging on slender stems as if to dry, four inches tall at most. We walked very slowly now, afraid of missing anything. I looked at Jane. She was smiling. We were hitting spring right on the target, and there were miles of it ahead of us.

The path was undulating now, in and out of small ravines cut by springs rising somewhere above us that trickled across our path. Fuller, noisier ones made us use steppingstones to cross them. Tucked in between these tiny watercourses and miniature waterfalls were brook lettuce and bluets, smallest of flowers, minute petals of sky blue with a yellow eye and leaves like drops of wet jade.

"Look!" Jane pointed over our heads.

We had been so engrossed in watching the ground that we had failed to notice the silverbell tree hanging over us, its white bells dangling in single file from the dark branches. I was beginning to feel slightly heady. Then, because I was leading this stretch, I saw the prize. Above us on the bank were thousands of trout lilies. I knelt down to see them better. Barely as high as my shoelaces, their tiny golden petals were swept back in dainty arcs, leaving the long brown stamens hanging below. Their leaves were mottled with blotches of paler green, supposedly resembling the scales of a trout. What could we say? Wildflower lovers understand each other. There are no words to describe such a scene. Here in this lost forest they bloom ten days at most, showing off their marvelous beauty to the bees and butterflies, then dry up and disappear underground to wait for another spring to tickle their hormones into action again.

"Out West we call them glacier lilies, because they follow right after the melting snow," I said, touching the petals gently.

We were so absorbed that we were unaware of a hiker waiting to pass us on the narrow trail. He was young, with a rough beard, and he carried a heavy backpack.

"Morning," he said, leaning on his hiking sticks, one in each hand. "Pretty sight," and he looked at the hillside of lilies.

We stood aside to let him pass. "Surely you're not headed for Maine?" Jane asked.

"That's right. All the way, if I'm lucky. Get there about September, I figure." He was friendly and confident.

"Going all alone?" I asked, knowing it was a foolish question.

He shifted his pack. "It's hard to find someone who walks like you do and can go when you can. Besides, I run into people every day, and at night, especially in the shelters."

"How far each day?" Jane asked. "And how about supplies?"

"I try to cover twenty miles. My mother drops off food packets every so many days ahead, by mail. I just have to keep on schedule."

He had it all figured out. We wished him well, and he was soon out of sight around a bend in the trail. I thought about his mother as I walked along, following his journey with a trail map and a good deal of anxiety for company, packing his "drops" of food. Mothers have it tough, loving so much.

Jane had stopped ahead of me, and I could tell by the way she waited for me, silently, there was something else to see. Before us was a hillside made in heaven. As far up as we could see, the steep slopes were covered with trillium, great white floppy heads of three-petalled lilies, three inches across, rising from three shiny leaves. Trillium grandiflorum. The largest of all the trilliums. It was a sight beyond words. Was it this way every spring, I asked myself, in this tucked-away mountain cove? Nothing else could match this sight. This day. This place. Whether we were overcome from too much beauty, or suddenly practical again, we decided to sit down in the middle of all this splendor and eat our lunch.

"I wonder if Andre Michaux ever came this way?" I asked Jane as we ate our sandwiches. "He discovered this trillium."

"Tell me about him," she said, leaning back against a log.

"You shouldn't get me started on him," I said, offering her a section of my orange. "Thirty years ago I sat in a terrible traffic jam while driving through Black Mountain, long before the interstate bypassed the town. I happened to be stalled beside an historical marker. It eulogized Michaux, describing him as a botanist who explored the Carolinas in 1785 for the king of France."

"That was really early. Why on earth did France care about what was growing in America?"

"The king wanted plants that would be suitable for Versailles. He commissioned Michaux, who was in charge of his gardens, to find them. Michaux wandered everywhere, for years, all over the east coast, even to Canada, discovering plants, gathering seeds, all for the king. Can you imagine our bluets at Versailles? He was a lonely, melancholy man who lost his wife when his only son was born. When the boy got to be fifteen he joined his father in America. I think about Michaux a lot when I walk these trails."

Perhaps I understand him, I thought to myself. The love of wildflowers and the plants of the deep woods monopolizes me too, and refreshes my spirit. Makes me not mind returning to an empty house when the day is over.

The wind had picked up while we were eating. The blue sky with which we began the day had disappeared.

"Listen," Jane said, her head to one side.

Far away we heard a drumming, a muffled sound like distant traffic. We knew what it was and quickly pulled our rain gear from our day packs. A wren flew across our path and into the bank to her hidden nest. She knew. There was a warning rumble of thunder, and then the wind made a great sucking sound and the air was filled with pollen and maple tassels and silverbells and huge raindrops. In minutes it became a downpour. Great Smoky Mountain weather, unpredictable as always! There was no choice but to hike on to the car we had left earlier at Lemon Gap.

No more wildflower adoration. No more conversation. Our heads were bent now against the driving rain, walking at a fast pace to keep warm. The rain made it difficult to see. We were preoccupied with staying dry and vertical. Our trail had become a streambed, and our eyes were on the hazards of rocks and roots under our feet and not on the sodden wildflowers around us. We spent another hour concentrating on our boots and how and where we should put them while the rain swept in great drenching gusts through our spring forest.

It was hard to describe the emotion engendered in our hearts by the metallic sheen on Jane's Chevrolet seen through the wet leaves of the forest that day. The car had its own kind of beauty. Suddenly we began to talk, to congratulate each other that the day had turned out so well, despite the storm. The rain, we agreed, had only given it extra zest, making us feel bold and invincible. As the rain tapered off, I saw another patch of "Dutchman's breeches," truly wet at last and hanging gamely on their tiny stems, waiting to dry in earnest now, given the chance. We drove home, contented with our day, passing the summit of Max Patch high above us. The storm clouds had split up into great fluffy pieces, scurrying away with the wind to other mountains and other hikers to do their work.

Random Thoughts on a Cloudy Day

F I didn't own a strong pair of legs I would be prone to melancholy. Walking leads me to new places of the spirit and restores me to good humor. Stepping through the wind, fog, and rain buoys me and drives away what could be a pervading sadness. Sadness that comes, perhaps, for things undone, words unsaid, places unvisited, and a wistfulness for time to do them. Whether the exercise or diversion does the job, I am almost always uplifted in mood when I return from my walk.

Each morning on arising I go out onto my porch to check the weather. I can look in four directions: north and east are limitless; west and south, the sky must be my judge as the forest closes me in. If all looks well, I hang out the hammock. In my bare feet, for the dew is heavy, I walk to the flowerbed to see what grew in last night's moonlight. Then there is breakfast to prepare and coffee to drink in the corner window where the sun touches first. There I make my plans for the day. If the day is dark and threatening and my mood uncertain, I take a walk.

Yesterday was one of those days. The sky was leaden, and the May temperature cool. I chose the Limby Birch hill and my "treasured path." There are many trails on my place. Some my children carved out of the forest with their hatchets and snippers long ago, mysterious little paths with crooked turns taken to avoid a log too big or a rhododendron thicket too dense to thin. These wandering ways always recall my children, who have grown up and left.

I remember the days they made their trails. Most often they were rainy days when other plans had to be put on hold for dryer weather. They wanted to surprise me. "Stay away, Mother, till we're done. Promise?" Hours passed while I busied myself inside, hearing the many trips they made back to the garage for tools, or to the refrigerator for sustenance. But I kept my promise, and later I would be led triumphantly to the woods to marvel at their work.

I stepped past the old log marking the beginning of one of these paths. This particular path had proven to be a useful cutoff to the Boundary Trail, which marks my property line with that of the Great Smoky Mountains National Park. I paused and held the branches aside to see the old gate in the woods. It had lain hidden for years until I discovered it on one of my wanderings, and hung on one hinge now. It was still solid and heavy and belonged to the chestnut-rail fence that wound for miles, marking the park boundaries. The fence had been a government labor project of the Depression, putting men to work, delineating park land from its neighbors. I am one of these neighbors, and it always gives me a thrill to step through the old gate and know I am on federal land, deeded to wilderness forever. But time has taken its toll on the old chestnut-rail fence, and much of it lies on the ground, broken by windfalls and age.

I paused by a decaying stump. It felt damp and spongy and had bits of moss and stonecrop growing in its core. This is the way it is in the Smokies. The excessive dampness turns a stump into a garden of growing things. This stump was three feet across, and my girls had danced on it years before when its surface was smoother and they were small. The chestnut stumps held magic for me. They were part of the ancient primeval forest that covered the mountains. The chestnuts are gone now, killed by a blight in the 1920s. Lumber companies made a fortune selling their wood as wormy chestnut paneling.

Stories about how it was in the "olden days" intrigue me. I've always liked the past better than the present. If I had my way I would have been one of those early settlers, wearing a calico sunbonnet and hoeing my tomatoes and watching my man build a log cabin dry and strong for us to live and love in.

I had reached the top of the Limby Birch hill. I never knew how or why it got this name, but my caretaker, Ernest, told me once there had been a giant birch tree here long ago, before his time, too.

The sky had turned threatening and the wind had picked up and tossed the treetops above me and sorted out old leaves left from last winter, sending them on another journey. Sometimes, when the children were small and fearful of the moaning in the trees, I told them that this was where the wind was made. "Right here, look up and you can tell." I sat them down on rocks and put my arms around them to listen. What a place this had been for them!

Before me now, just off the trail, was a small grassy spot of velvet green. It was always this way, except when snow covered it, a spot of beguiling beauty, an island of green softness in the middle of the forest. I used to bring the children here. It was just far enough for them to walk when they were little. We sat on the grass and I told them stories about fawns lying here too sometimes and resting. Why did the grass grow so soft and high here and nowhere else in the woods, I'd ask them? The mystery intrigues me still. I walked on.

I love the woods before the new leaves appear. In May the sun is able to reach the early wildflowers just peeping out on the forest floor and hurry them on to bloom before the dense shade takes over. Most precious of all of these to me were the wild lilies of the valley. I searched the ground for the telltale leaves, two long fleshy ovals opposite each other on a skinny stem. There they were. I bent down to see the delicate spray of white bells hidden under one of the leaves. There were two weeks in the year when they bloomed; miss that and I'd wait another year. There were dozens of them now on either side of the trail.

Perhaps that is why I've called this my "treasured path." James Nolan from down in the valley came to do some carpentry for me some years back. We found we both loved the mountains and the seasons the same way. He asked me one day, "Do you need any help outside?" I remember taking him to see the old trails, some impassable from fallen trees. "Just tell me what you want done," he told me, "and I'll do it." James restored my trails "with love," I told my friends when they came to hike them. He kept the old twists and turns and never removed a mossy log or a handsome branch if it looked pretty. He just expected me to step over it or bend down a bit, which I did.

I have him to thank for opening up the spring. I had reached it now and stopped to listen. I could hear a faint but steady trickling under the wind sound. The land dropped down steeply now, and ferns and lichen grew everywhere on the logs and rocks. Below me, through the leaves, I could see a thin glistening of water. James had cleaned up the bank where the spring trickled out, and now I could step close to

it and put my fingers in the cold rivulets seeping out of the soil. I thought about springs as I knelt there. Raindrops from a passing storm over my mountain started this one. How many years before? Sinking deeply, silently, into the earth, raindrops plotted their own dark travels underground, finding their own subterranean highways of rocky fissures and watery tunnels, down, down, seeking an exit somewhere and finding it here at last in my spring.

I had many springs on the property, each in its own setting. A tiny notch between two hills marked one, a thick grouping of maples and hemlocks giving it away. Another lay in a flat area by a rhododendron thicket, the strongest spring on the property, I was told, but gone before my time. Cows pastured on the property for many years had trampled it back into its hole. Many times I dug in vain to recapture it, but it needed stronger help than mine to free it from its muddy seal.

I could tell I was nearing the meadow, for the light had increased and the trees were thinning. The trail would soon end. I wasn't really ready in spirit for it to be over. The wind moaned louder. It would rain soon. Then I caught my breath. I leaned closer over a patch of brush in the damp undergrowth. A spike of lavender had pierced through the jumble of twigs to catch the light. It was a purple-fringed orchid. Dozens of miniature orchid faces with shredded violet petals grew on the slender stem, maybe twelve inches high. They are very rare. I had studied the orchid's picture a dozen times in my wildflower book, wishing I might be lucky enough to find one on my place. The years passed and I had never seen one. But, then, I had never been here at this spot during this particular week before. There was another, behind the first, and to the side, three others. Suddenly I felt rich. My heart soared. Gone was my melancholy, blown away on the cold spring wind.

Meadow Friends

ONE OF the rewards of owning land is learning what lies hidden in its soil—noticing what appears one spring and disappears another. Why does Solomon's seal grow in the north meadow and not the south one? Why did an orange-fringed orchid appear last year in the same spot after a four-year absence? Even after thirty years of ownership of my North Carolina mountain farm, surprises await me each year. Plants have timetables of their own, I've learned, schedules dependent on sunlight, moisture, soil, and temperature.

Creeping Cedar I remember the day I discovered a strange little club moss growing on my property. November frosts had already nipped my mountain farm, turning the meadows a chilly beige. I poked around on this particular day, walking in a lonely corner I don't often visit, trying to keep warm, searching the ground, always looking for something new I might have missed on warmer days when there was so much else to see.

At eye level, in the brittle grass of an old road bank, I suddenly noticed a lush green ground cover spreading about under a mountain laurel. Its miniature cedar-like fronds made springy green nests wherever they ran. The moss had the endearing quality of making you want to pet it, which I did, reaching up and feeling its starchy little branches, pleasant and cheery on this bleak winter day. On an impulse I gave it a yank, and up came three feet of emerald runners dangling in my hand. Shallow-rooted, it had no trouble traveling wherever it wanted to go, independent of all things but its own wild ways.

"Creeping cedar" or "running pine," the mountain people call it, completely inaccurate but appealing "folk names." Lycopodium is not even vaguely related to pines or cedars. No doubt its evergreen, frond-like texture inspired such titles.

Its club moss ancestors grew 130 feet high, along with towering ferns and horsetails. Club mosses formed part of the great carboniferous forests 300 million years ago, when the world was young and there were vast stretches of warm tropical seas and little temperature change. This was a time when great amphibian reptiles lolled in the warm swamps and nibbled at the lower branches of monster plants like my little Lycopodium.

I found my moss in many places the following spring. Sun or shade made no difference to "creeping cedar." At Caldwell Fork, a thousand feet below my property, in the Great Smoky Mountain National Park, I found half an acre covering an old home site, running in and out of the scattered chimney stones. Another day, closer to the house, I discovered a bed in full sunshine hidden in the deep grass. I had simply failed to notice. My neighbors like to see it in their family cemeteries. I can understand that. There is a cheeriness about its wandering habits, turning a sad heart into acceptance, watching its tiny green mats creep over the graves in its own time.

But try to transplant it! After thirty years of living in one place in the summer, I thought my garden soil beside the house finally acceptable to the wild things I found in the woods. "Creeping cedar" refused to accommodate me. After buckets of wood's earth and loving care, the runners I had so carefully buried never became attached to the soil, but turned yellow and died. I've learned a lot about transplanting—mainly to forget it unless you can give your wild plant exactly what it wants. There's a lot going on in that black mountain dirt, earthy relationships between roots and fungi you can't see and perhaps don't know about. Symbiosis is what the Greeks called it, meaning "with life." Unless you can manage setting up that arrangement, forget it. I've learned the hard way. After years of disappointment, I visit my wild friends where they like to live and leave them in peace.

•

Bee Balm For want of something better to do on a lazy summer afternoon while drifting back and forth in my hammock, watching the clouds, I try to pick my favorite month for wildflowers. That's a tough assignment in the Smokies. May has its ardent supporters for trillium and spring beauties. Others pick June, when the mountain laurel turns the ridgetops pink and flame azaleas light up the forests with orange fire. Perhaps July, when the purple rhododendron bloom. But give me August. Bee balm blooms in August—great colonies of it six feet tall, with Raggedy Ann mops of cheery scarlet petals sticking out in all directions, looking so disheveled and comical they make me smile.

Sun lover, shade lover, lover of bogs, bee balm thrives when its roots are damp. A member of the vast mint family, it has that family's characteristics: square stems, aromatic, opposite leaves with a flush of red where the leaf joins the stem. Bee balm's first cousins, some call them horse-mints, grow in my meadows too, in all colors from pale lavender to deep purple.

Bee balm has other names: ragged robin, mountain mint, wild bergamot. John Bartram, one of America's first plant explorers, named it Oswego tea back in the eighteenth century, when he found the Indians around Lake Ontario brewing a tonic from its leaves. Despite its name, it's rather a difficult plant for bees to handle because it doesn't provide any "landing platform" for them to rest on. Bee balm is friendlier to hummingbirds and butterflies, who like its red color and can plunge their tongues down the dozens of long scarlet throats of the flower head to find nectar. I expect the Oswego Indians learned it made a good salve for bee stings and passed the information along, giving bee balm its name.

Bartram gave bee balm the botanical name of *Monarda didyma*. Monarda for Nicholas Monardes. Didyma, Greek for "twin stamens," which protrude out of each scarlet bugle. Nicholas Monardes was an eminent physician and botanist who lived in Seville between 1590 and 1688, heady years for Spain, which claimed ownership of all lands west of the Cape Verde Islands. Seville, already a city of great culture and renown, with access to the Mediterranean, was suddenly on the cutting edge of the trade flowing from the New World back to the Old. What excited Monardes was the wealth of exotic flora that came back to Spain in the great sailing ships. He thrilled over the potential medicinal values the specimens might have. He wrote two volumes entitled *Joyful News from the New Found World*, though he never set foot in the vast wilderness across the ocean he praised so highly. Botanists often named their discoveries after well-known men who had no connection with their finds. Bartram discovered *Monarda didyma* fifty years after Monardes died, naming it after him and making him immortal as far as wildflower lovers are concerned.

So vases of bee balm brighten up my house in August, and it enlivens the meadows outside and anywhere where mountain springs keep the ground moist. It takes a hard-hearted person not to soften when he passes it, seeing it standing bold and bright off the shoulder of the county road.

Joe-Pye-weed An endearing name, Joe-Pye-weed. An intimate, friendly name. I wandered down my mountain road in late August to see Joe growing seven feet tall off in the ditch, his lacy pink dome of a hundred tiny flowers bowing to every breeze, welcoming bees by the score to enjoy his vanilla-like perfume. Where were you yesterday, Joe-Pye, that I failed to notice you growing among all the hundreds of weeds by my roadside? How did you get so tall so fast, and where was I? This happens to me every year. I'm always surprised Joe arrives without much fanfare, tall and lanky and nondescript until he blooms. Then he's splendid and regal, towering above his humbler companions.

Named for Joe Pye, an Indian witch doctor who practiced his trade in the time of the Pilgrims, old Joe cured people of typhoid fever by making concoctions from Joe-Pye-weed's roots and florets. The herb was used for other ailments too. Joe-Pye's efficacy covered everything from improving the complexion to kidney disorders. A tonic made from the leaves could soothe the nerves. It always surprises me that Indians were prone to civilized aches and pains like we are. I'm steeped in myths, expecting our native peoples to have been always strong and healthy from outdoor living and not tempted towards appetite loss or the vagaries of disposition that beset us.

Joe-Pye-weed is a harbinger of fall. When he appears in my meadows, apples already hang on the apple trees. Highbush blueberries are ripe, and bears are competing with me to harvest them. Blackberries, too, are purple and tasty, and my objection to them and their scratchy brambles that spread in all directions across the waving grasses eases a bit when I eat one. I startled a mother grouse yesterday in one patch, and her roaring flight out of the thicket alarmed me until I saw her babies waddle one by one across my path, and she calling pitifully from the opposite side to distract me, feigning a broken wing. I wonder about the hunters and their hounds who will come once I am gone. I don't bother with "no trespassing" signs. Hunters will come anyway, knowing the land as well as I and feeling that it's half theirs after so many generations of living next door to it.

Joe-Pye tells me each year that it's almost time to leave, that my summer on the Cataloochee Divide is over. Cooler nights and clear skies and a touch of frost on the outside bench is waiting for me when I wake up each morning to hasten me with my packing. Down the road I'll drive one day soon for the last time, stopping at a curve where I can look back and see the house and the land it sits upon and whisper "Goodbye for a while." And Joe? He's turned to a dried-up stalk of nothing, retreating into himself, regrouping, storing his energies down in the dusty ground for another August.

The Gazebo

'VE SEEN lots of places called home in my summers here in the Great Smoky Mountains of North Carolina. I've seen settlers' cabins made of chestnut logs, still tight and dry after a hundred years, and a rock chimney built so finely that not a curl of smoke could find its way out the cracks. I've seen a stone house with a sod roof, pitched on a slope so steep that it was a hop, skip, and jump for the sheep to climb up and nibble lunch. I've seen an A-frame with a twenty-foot window catching its own little mountain in the glass and holding it like a jewel. I've seen trailer homes whose owners loved them so well they dressed them up with wooden porches and trellises and brick chimneys. But trailers are only trailers to me, and they still shiver and shake when you walk inside them. Yet in all my wanderings in these lonesome woods and high meadows, I never thought I'd find folks living in a gazebo. That's right, a gazebo, one of those octagonal teahouses our great-grandmothers fancied out on a lawn somewhere by the sea. No walls, no doors, just wooden arches and curlicues and a fancy cupola where the roof comes to a point. A gazebo in the wilderness!

I was back in my cabin for three months, spending my usual summer afternoon in my Pauley's Island rope hammock, swaying back and forth, not really reading though I was holding a book, just barely moving, watching the mountains around me disappear then reappear in the afternoon haze. No company, just myself, and loving every minute of it. My nearest neighbor lives a mile away. We're summer folk who live here on the Cataloochee Divide. We see each other three times a year. I like that, and guess they do too. Nothing's changed, either, in thirty years. Not them, not me. Oh we've all aged, and my husband's gone now, but I'm still the same.

I had a scare, though, long ago. The land below me, a track called the Big Laurel, had been surveyed, and one day as I walked the boundary line on my northern side, I saw orange ribbons tied to the trees, dozens of them marking off homesites. Days later I heard a bulldozer tearing up the forest, building a road. Then nothing else happened. The project sat. Nobody came, nobody bought. The new road became a fine grassy trail for me to walk on and look for jacks-in-the-pulpit. A few orange ribbons fluttered about on the trees. I grew complacent. Years passed.

Any noise is noticeable at my place. The 2:00 P.M. plane from Knoxville to Asheville was right on time. It was lost in the blue, right over my head. A bobwhite on the fence called out his two-pitch whistle. Other than that, there was just the usual grasshopper-and-cricket drone that goes with summer. Then I heard the whine of a chainsaw. I sat straight up, and my book fell onto the grass. The sound was close. Too close. My heart skipped about as I tried to figure out where it was coming from. I pinned it down to the forest below the Knob. The saw stopped. Then it started again as its owner moved to another tree. I ran inside and put on my hiking boots. I was going to have a neighbor at long last. Close by. Who was he? Where was he?

In no time I was on my way. It was easy following that high-pitched whine through the woods. I dove through thickets of rhododendron like a dog on a scent. It didn't matter to me that the going was heavy. I had a quest. In minutes I stumbled upon a path outlined with pebbles all the same size. It was a pretty path, like one a child would make, curving around mossy logs and a bed of pink lady slipper orchids. I'd never seen lady slippers on my property. The path led me to a pile of firewood, all neatly stacked according to size, and a campfire circle ringed with rocks. My heart was thawing a little.

The saw had stopped. I didn't need it, anyway, because I was there. I had reached a clearing in the woods and saw a kind of pavilion, like a bandstand, half-finished, of bright new lumber, with eight sides and five people sitting in it or on it, drinking beer. One was strumming a guitar. They looked like they might all burst into song until I came out of the woods and startled them. I suppose I looked like an apparition to them, my white hair tangled with twigs from the low branches I had crawled under.

"Hello," I said rather apologetically. "I'm your neighbor. I heard the saw." I smiled at them, thinking how young they looked. But mostly I looked at the structure they were building. It was all arches and lattice work, roofless, and about twelve feet in diameter. They must have been building it for some time before I returned for the summer.

A young man stood up. "I'm Pete," he said, climbing over the low wall of the stand and holding out his hand. "Come in, come in, we're taking a break. Have a beer?"

I shook my head, stepping carefully over a pile of lumber. "This is the first time I've heard of you. You've done a lot." I really meant it. I tried not to show how dumbfounded I was over the incongruity of this delicate structure plopped right in the middle of one of the deepest of Appalachian forests. Specimen trees towered over its delicate wood-work. One thick branch could fall and smash its pretty sides in an afternoon breeze.

"Where are you all from?"

"Florida," Pete said, as he put his arm around one of the young women, whose blond hair was tucked under a scarf. "Meet my wife, Jenny."

Jenny and I shook hands. "That's a long way to come."

"We wait for a long weekend. We need three days to make it worthwhile. I guess you wonder what we're building?" he looked at me, waiting for my comments.

I had to go carefully. I felt pretty old and out of touch with this group.

"It's going to be mighty pretty. What is it?"

Pete bent over and from a dusty pile of plans and papers in a corner pulled out a much-handled newspaper photograph.

"Jenny saw this picture in our Sunday paper a year ago," he said, and he handed it to me eagerly.

I was looking at a real, bona fide gazebo, a white lacy teahouse with eight romantic arches and a roof rising to an elaborate point at the top with a finial capped with a golden ball. No glass, no doors, no screens, just an adorable wooden wedding cake was what it looked like, and the happy couple not on top, but standing here in front of it,

facing me, and waiting for me to add my enthusiasm to theirs.

I had to pick my words. I had seen it rain an inch an hour last June, and the lightning storms were memorable. "The main thing is to be comfortable," I said. "And you're doing a fantastic job of following that picture," I added, looking at the photograph I was holding.

The others seemed to relax a bit, and the young man with the guitar plucked a chord.

"We had just bought this lot when Jenny saw the picture. We fell in love with it and sent off for the plans," Pete said. "Jeff and Gordon and Jo are helping us when we get time off from work." He included all of them in his ready smile.

The others nodded. I could see they were all dedicated to the project.

We were youth versus age—youth refusing to worry about dampness and windstorms, age eager to be prepared and ready for the worst.

He seemed to read my mind. "Of course, we've got a tent if it comes to that, and we can stow our gear under the floor here," and he pointed to a nicely built storage area under the gazebo.

I thought of my closets, my attic, my garage. My house!

"You know," he continued, "we've had the most extraordinary luck. It hasn't rained—hard that is—since we started building." Pete looked at the others and they all nodded their heads.

"You were born under a lucky star," I said. Perhaps optimism drove off rainstorms and insects. I needed more of it. It was time to get off the teahouse subject before I asked something really practical. "Your path through the woods is charming. It's easy to tell you love it here."

"Wait till next spring," Jenny said. "We've planted a hundred tulips up the road."

"You won't have any bears or deer eating those," I said, thinking how extra-civilized tulips would look in this wild forest. Well, their enthusiasm was getting to me. I needed to go home.

"Come visit me if you ever take time off," I said, standing up to go.

"You all come back," Pete said.

It was another year before I even thought of the gazebo again. Winter had brought with it a severe bout with flu, and I felt for the first time my own mortality through the long weeks of recuperation. I yearned for my cabin in the mountains. By summer I was back again, sweeping out winter's reminders: spiders and mice that had made the cabin their home for nine months, old leaves trapped under porch benches; putting out the cushions. I love the rituals of opening up. They mean I am back for another three months of summer. I worked away with my broom, making the place all mine once more.

One day after settling in, my afternoon walk led me near the gazebo area, and I thought about my young neighbors and wondered how they had fared through the winter with their project. I could see their new road with the sunlight on it through the trees and decided to have a look. I walked up the road with the remains of their tulips lining the way. There was no car in sight.

"Anyone at home?" I called out, not wanting to surprise them. I passed a small green tent placed off to one side in a laurel thicket. I guessed from its size and discreet location it must be the privy. Further on I came to a neat campsite with a brand-new nylon tent. Through the opening I could see two sleeping bags on beds of hemlock boughs. No one home there, either. Then I saw the gazebo.

For a cynic who loves her comfort, I was enchanted. They had chosen to stain it natural instead of painting it white as in the picture, and it had a kind of amber glow about it. The eight arches were outlined now with wooden leaves. Above them were double cornices with an intricate series of miniature friezes that ran around the entire octagon. Every wooden detail of ornamentation available in woodworking catalogues had been studied and selected carefully. The finial, a globe of carved wood painted gold, topped off this wooden masterpiece. Neat rolls of mosquito netting had been installed inside each of the arches, ready to roll down if needed. Gear was stowed in corners neatly and underneath the floor. A Carolina jasmine vine was being trained to climb up a pillar, and one yellow bloom showed it was thriving.

Then I saw their view. I had been away so many months that I hadn't heard the saw cutting out this window in their forest. They had topped dozens of trees, pruned others, and now they could sit in their teahouse and see the far-off mountains and valleys and what was in between. The view was choice. The building was glorious. I wanted to leave them a note telling them I had been there. I found a pad on top of some gear and wrote: "You've done it. Congratulations!" and anchored it with a rock at their entrance.

I walked home thinking hard about what they had accomplished by themselves. It was their way of making their land their own. I admired them, but wondered about the vaguely dissatisfied feeling I felt inside. I poured myself a drink and went out on my porch to analyze what was going on in my mind. Looking at the mountains had helped me solve many a problem over the years. What was it? Coming to the truth, I was downright jealous, that's what it was. I was envious of their little teahouse. That was exactly it. I had a thought. Could I, perhaps, borrow their plans and look them over? One could never tell; a gazebo might look just fine over there beyond the hammock at the edge of the lawn.

Bobwhite

THE BOBWHITE is a shy bird and hard to see. His feathers are the color of dry grass except for a white stripe up the back of his head. He likes to sit on my split-rail fence and sing out his name in the early morning and evening. It's quiet then. Sometimes his song has awakened me from sleep, and I have stolen outside on the damp porch in my nightgown, with the sun barely up, searching for him. His call persistent, tantalizingly close.

"Bobwhite!"

There, I have spotted him. On the lower rail his stout little body sits, not moving a feather, singing out his message. He likes this stretch of fence very well, it seems, a perch from which he commands my east meadow and house. Last evening, younger eyes than mine picked him out more quickly. His call caught a space between our voices and the grandchildren stopped their chattering to look for him.

"Bobwhite!"

You have captured us all, Bob White. Interrupted our thoughts. Two notes, one high, one low, and you are done for a while. What are you calling?

I sink quietly into a porch chair, alone this August evening at last, bone-tired, feeling my seventy-five years and the strains and joys of different generations under one roof. My eyes half-closed, I lean my head back, listening, and feeling the soft wind that blows on the grasses in the meadow. Beyond the meadow, the misty mountains of the Smokies line up, ridge after ridge, disappearing into the usual Appalachian haze of summer.

The guests are gone, the screen door slammed for the last time this summer by a child searching for a jar for the ladybug she cradles in her hand. I have only the mountains for company now and the goldfinches, who love my black thistle seed in the feeder hanging by the window. And you, Bob White, to fill the few days left to me here with your song. Joe-Pye-weed is growing tall, and goldenrod fills the pastures, a sign of fall.

A wistfulness accompanies the subtle change from summer to fall. A feeling of turning inward, a regrouping of one's energies, not unlike the buds on the white oaks, closed tight and waiting to take the place of the dry leaves about to fall. Or Queen Anne's lace out in the meadow: its flat flowerhead curls up on itself now, becoming a dry tangle of wispy seedheads. There are premonitions all around me. Hurry with your goodbyes, they say. Time flies.

I have strange goodbyes to make. I still collect treasures, something new each summer I haven't seen before. Last month I spotted a monster chestnut stump, all but hidden by blackberry brambles. To me, passing a chestnut stump is like passing a consecrated spot. The time of the chestnuts is gone forever from this land. Old stumps sprout, but the new growth soon succumbs to the blight that killed the parent. Above my house in the second-growth forest are many stumps, mostly hidden now by briars and heavy undergrowth. I live in a temperate rainforest, almost a mile high, where an inch of rain an hour is not unusual. My stump measured eight hands across, as best I could tell, with the blackberry prickles scratching at my arms as I measured. I looked around and counted others, some not as large, scattered about. I stood in the remains of a primeval forest. What was happening in this land as my chestnut grew thick and tall? Surely it saw Indians gathering its nuts and the white settlers who followed them looking for prime farming land. My farm would have suited them very well, with alfalfa and apple trees and potatoes liking the black soil and the sunny, cool days. So I must scramble once more through the blackberries to see my stump before I go.

Echo Rock would merit a goodbye too. It sits out in the middle of the big meadow below the house. Wild cherries with their shiny ma-

hogany bark rise out of its tumbled slabs of granite. On a picnic decades ago we found an echo here, my children and I, as we heard our
voices bouncing back to us suddenly from the nearby hills.

I have witnessed all seasons here. I have seen the hardwoods on the
meadow's edge turn to reds and golds, and after the December wind has
done its work, watched it send the leaves spinning in furious circles
round and round, tossing them high in the sky and catching them
again, pressing them into brown heaps in the ditches of my road. I have
seen the silhouettes of winter when the apple trees stand bare, their fruit
unpicked, hanging like rubies in the cold, clear air, waiting for frosts to
turn them brown and dry until they fall, too, and join the dry leaves.
And spring? What a morning May brought me once, when the serviceberry trees along my road, already white with blossoms, turned to spar-
kling glass in a late freeze. I remember that old mountain caution: "Wait
until Mother's Day before planting." That was Mother's Day.

"Bobwhite!"

It is like stirring the soup pot, sitting here, communicating with
Bobwhite and musing about my land. Memories rise up like bubbles out
of the depths of my remembering. I see my children again running
down the grasses to the swing hanging from the black locust tree, telling
me later they swung higher than the mountains around them. And those
June days of strawberry picking. We savored the best of the land then,
walking the mountainsides looking for the sweet red berries in the high
grass, hiding beneath their leaves. We'd cap them gently and drop them
in the tin pots each of us carried. Making jam took a lot of berries. Later, when the berries bubbled in their sugar juice on the stove, everyone
who picked stood around watching and taking turns stirring, their hours
of picking to be rewarded with the taste of jam on newly baked bread.

And Sara? When she came each summer for her mountain visit, we
were more like sisters than friends. Sitting on the window seat, she and I,
long past midnight, the moon our only light, we talked about love and
husbands. Women can always talk about love! Moonlight is a purveyor of
confidence. Once we watched foxes on the lawn dancing in the twilight.
Each night for a week they came between eight and nine while we stood
silent by the window, watching, marveling at our luck to see silver foxes
close up. She is gone now, too young, from those who loved her.

The moon is a companion here. It rises out of an ocean of mountain mist and suddenly appears full-blown, rosy still with sunset, right off the porch, without notice. Then my guests draw up their chairs and put their feet on the porch rail. An intimacy draws all of us together in the darkness, and we talk of many things as we watch the moon climb its path. The blackness in the meadow beyond the fence is filled with fireflies, and the stars shine more brightly on this lonely

mountain. A satellite joins the stars on its own secret man-made course. There are nights when I awaken too early. Last night was one of them. It was 2:00 A.M., and worrying that I had sleepless hours ahead of me, I watched the moon rise beyond my window. It was just a crescent of itself this week, but was comforting and soporific, and I slept again.

I know now, Bob White, what you are calling: that I have you forever and all other things I love here.

I got up and walked down the lawn to where I last heard his call. He had flown away while I was resting. I touched the rail he had sat upon and, bending down, picked up a feather he had left behind. I walked back to the house feeling its downy softness between my fingers. It was as light as air. Going inside I dropped it into my open suitcase.